The Overcomer's Handbook

A Collection of Confessions, Meditations, Prayers, and Insightful Biblical Truths

The Overcomer's Handbook

A collection of confessions, meditations, prayers, and insightful Biblical Truths

> "This book of the Law shall not depart from your mouth. But you shall meditate therein day and night, and observe to do all that is written in it, and you shall make your way prosperous and have good success."
> (Joshua 1:8)

Pastor Ian M. Taylor

THE OVERCOMER'S HANDBOOK

Cover Design by Justin Taylor, Ian Taylor Ministries Inc.

© Copyright 2008

SAINT PAUL PRESS, DALLAS, TX
IAN TAYLOR MINISTRIES INC.

First Printing, 2008

All rights reserved. No part of this publication may be reproduced, stored in a retrieval system, or transmitted in any form or by any means, electronic, mechanical, photocopying, recording, or otherwise, without the prior permission of the copyright owner, except for brief quotations included in a review of the book.

Most scripture quotations are taken from the King James Version, New King James, and Amplified versions of the Bible. However, many other translations have been used separately or combined to clarify and expound on the meaning of the Scriptures, or to give the reader a better understanding of the subject of study. In addition, Scripture verses have been paraphrased by the author all throughout the book.

The name SAINT PAUL PRESS and its logo are registered as a trademark in the U.S. patent office.

ISBN-10: 0-9817520-7-1
ISBN-13: 978-0-9817520-7-5

Printed in the USA

DEDICATION

To all believers who desire to have the victory of the resurrection manifested in their lives.

THE OVERCOMER'S HANDBOOK
Table Of Contents

Introduction..19

1. Section I - Insightful Biblical Truths
   (Psalm 19:18)..25

   A. The Majesty of God's Word...............................27
   B. Think On These Things......................................28
   C. The Word, The Word, The Word.......................29
   D. The Word Is Your Life..30
   E. The absolute importance of your confession...30
   F. Biblical Meditation: The Master Key
      for Success..40
   G. Provoking Thoughts on Prayer.........................47
   H. Total identification: Based on the Perfect
      Substitutionary Works of Christ.......................51
   I. The Power of Thanksgiving................................53
   J. The Power of Rejoicing.......................................55
   K. Why Tithe?...58
   L. What is the Principle of Tithing?......................60
   M. 21 Reasons To Tithe..63

2. Section II - Confessions (Romans 3:4)..................67

   A. Redemptive Truths (John 8:32).........................69
      1. Redemption..71
      2. Portrait of the new man................................71
      3. The reality of redemption.............................73
      4. Redemption is mine.......................................74
      5. Put on the new man.......................................76
      6. Total identification confession....................77
      7. My true identity...79

8. Christ my life...80
9. Reality of righteousness.......................................81
10. Righteous consciousness....................................82
11. Realities of the new creation.............................83
12. Free in Jesus' Name...84

B. The Blood of Christ (Hebrews 13:20-21)...................87
1. The Blood of Christ..89
2. Because of the Blood of Christ............................90
3. Discerning the Blood of Christ............................92
4. Thanksgiving because of the Blood...................95

C. My Walk with God (Amos 3:3).....................................99
1. Do all in the name of Jesus...............................101
2. Live right, do right..101
3. Come up higher..102
4. My Christian walk (based on scripture that speaks of 'always' and 'never')..........103
5. Being led by the Spirit.......................................106
6. My Conscience..108
7. Diligence—Part 1...110
8. Diligence—Part 2...115
9. My Walk with God..116
10. God My Father..117

D. Victorious Living (1 Corinthians 15:57)................119
1. Overcomers..121
2. The fight of faith...122
3. This is what I believe...123
4. Spirit of Victory...124
5. I refuse to fear...126
6. Reaping with Joy..128
7. Free from shame..130
8. My Soul will Bless the Lord...............................131
9. Filled with His fullness......................................131

    10. The anointing in me 133
    11. Today's resolution 134
    12. Trust in Jehovah 136
    13. The Word and I 137
    14. His matchless name 138
    15. The name of Jesus 140
    16. Deliverance from pornography 142
    17. The anointing 143
    18. God's love in me 144

E. Talk Right (Proverbs 18:21) 147
    1. Right talk is Heavenly 149
    2. I Speak Life 150
    3. I Talk Right 151
    4. God's Word in my mouth 152

F. Redemptive Rights (Ephesians 1:3, 7) 153

    1. Healing:
       a. Healing is mine 155
       b. Healing confession 156
       c. I am healed 157

    2. Protection:
       a. Divine Protection 158

    3. Prosperity:
       a. My needs are met 159
       b. Financial deliverance 159
       c. Financial prosperity 161
       d. Remaining Steadfast in Prosperity 162
       e. Established in prosperity 163
       f. Restoration 165
       g. Tithing confession 165

      h. Money comes to me because...............166
      i. Eight financial nuggets..........................168
      j. Sowing and God's prosperity system...170

   4. My Children:
      a. My children—Part 1...............................171
      b. My children—Part 2...............................172
      c. I believe for me and my house............175

G. From the Psalms (Psalm 40:3)...........................177

   1. Prayers, Confessions, Meditations:
      a. Victory and comfort from the Psalms...179
      b. Praise from the Psalms..........................180
      c. My commitment to praise.....................186

   2. From Psalm 119:
      a. The Fear of the Lord...............................187
      b. My relationship with the Word............189
      c. "But and yet," nevertheless I stay
         with the Word..190
      d. "I make a quality decision"....................191
      e. Prayer for understanding......................192
      f. Prayer for personal revival....................193
      g. Prayers from Psalms 119.......................193

H. Short Confessions (Job 22:28):..........................197
   1. Miscellaneous confessions........................199
   2. Financial confessions.................................208
   3. Love confessions...216
   4. New creation confessions.........................217
   5. Prayer Life Confessions.............................221
   6. Minister's confession..................................223

3. **Section III – Prayers (Luke 18:1)** 229

   A. General Prayers (James 5:16b) 231
      1. Prayer Guide Based on
         the Lord's Prayer 233
      2. Spiritual insight & maturity 239
      3. Discerning The Blood of Christ 242
      4. Spiritual momentum 244
      5. Consecration 245
      6. Repentance 246
      7. Sanctification 247
      8. A perfect heart 247
      9. The fear of the Lord 250
      10. Open doors 251
      11. The unsaved 252
      12. Prayer keys from James 5:16 254

   B. Prayers for Pastors (Ephesians 6:19) 257
      1. Pastor's prayer 259
      2. Prayer for your church 260
      3. What to pray for Pastors and Leaders 261
      4. Go to church expecting 268

4. **Section IV – Biblical Meditations**
   (I Timothy 4: 15) 271

      1. Healing scriptures 273
      2. Prosperity scriptures 275
      3. Names for believers 277
      4. Miscellaneous scripture 279

5. **Section V – Conclusion (Ecclesiastes 12:13)**...............283

    A. Food for thought..285
    B. Final Word...291
    C. My Prayer for You...294

Prayer for Salvation...294

Personal Invitation..296

Resources..298

ACKNOWLEDGEMENTS

A virtuous and God-fearing wife is a blessing from the Lord. Daad, I am so blessed to have you as my wife and friend. Thank you for your thoughtful contributions to this book, for your persistence, and for your tireless labour of love. I admire your unwavering commitment to God.

Thanks to my daughter, Alicia, for her typing contribution; to my son, Justin, for designing the cover of this book; to the rest of my family for their encouragement and support for all that I set my hands to.

Thanks also to the many ministers of the Gospel who do not know me personally but who have had a significant impact on my spiritual life: Kenneth and Gloria Copeland, Kenneth E. Hagin, Norval Hayes, Frederick Price, Creflo Dollar, Leroy Thompson, Benny Hinn, Marilyn Hickey, Bill Winston, Keith Moore, Gary Whetstone, Joy Dawson, Charles Capps, and several others.

Most of all, I thank the Holy Spirit who teaches me all things and brings to my remembrance all things that I have need of.

INTRODUCTION

In 1996, the Lord impressed upon my heart to begin to write confessions on subjects relevant to believers' maturity. I was to gather them together over a period of time and compile them in a book called **The Overcomer's Handbook**. So this book has been in the making for a long time.

The Overcomer's Handbook is a collection of insightful biblical truths, confessions, meditations and prayers. The objective of this book is to put some of the necessary tools for total success in a simple and practical way so that you can begin to apply them immediately.

I believe that the information contained in this book, when acted upon, will cause you to have victory and success manifested in every area of your life. You can have total victory manifested spiritually, mentally, emotionally, physically, financially, and socially. It is your born again right and privilege to live in victory. God has given to you all things that pertain to life and godliness so that you can always triumph in Christ Who always enables you. Christ has obtained a perfect redemption for you. The fullness of God is available to you. God's plan for your life is victory and total success. No matter what has happened in your life, God's grace is abundant and sufficient for you to be totally successful.

Most believers are living far below their redemptive right and privileges. The times you and I are living in are difficult times. Most Christians are either too busy, or lack the motivation to invest the time necessary to operate effectively in God's system, which is the Kingdom of God.

This Christian self-help book is designed to help you to operate in the Kingdom of God and live out Kingdom of God principles.

The Bible teaches that there will be a shaking, and those things that are not properly aligned to the Kingdom of God will crumble. This world's financial system is destined to collapse. Now is the time for you to be rightly aligned to God's system, so that you will be able to stand and be victorious regardless of what happens around you.

The Overcomer's Handbook is tailored to help equip you for the times you are in, and the times to come. Joshua 1:8 tells us how we can make our way prosperous and have good success in every area of our lives. It states that we are to continually meditate, confess, and obey God's Word, and Proverbs 4:7 adds, "get understanding." This book teaches you how to meditate on God's Word, and provides an abundance of scriptures and truths, on which you ought to meditate. It is also filled with long and short Word-based confessions for various relevant areas of your life. You can receive understanding in several significant areas so that you may obtain revelation knowledge that will produce motivation for you to take the right actions on God's Word. This book will help you to think right, talk right, act right, walk in love, develop a prayer life, and walk in purity. Psalm 50:23 declares that when you conduct yourself correctly, God's salvation will be manifested.

The fullness of God and His Kingdom are in you. However, you must take the right steps to work out your salvation so that it may manifest. This book is a Christian manual that gives you the right steps to possess what is yours in Christ. This is more than just a book to read and put aside. This book should become a daily companion for you as a study guide and devotion.

To get the most out of this book do the following things:

1. Approach this book prayerfully. Allow the Holy Spirit to use this book to shine the light on the areas in your life where you need to focus, correct or come up higher.
2. This is your book; underline scriptures and thoughts that speak to you.
3. Get a separate notebook and make notes.
4. Use your Bible, and take the time to study scripture references.
5. Use this book daily and constantly until its truths become automatic in your life.
6. To maximize the effectiveness of this handbook in your life, I ask you to dissect the individual confessions, prayers , and articles. Consider what specific actions you need to take in thought, word, and deed in order to put into practice the truths found in each specific section.

Warning: Do not make the mistake of assuming that, because you understand the principles or have memorized the verses of Scripture, that victory will automatically follow. It is acting on God's Word that brings the right results. It is the truth that you continually practice that will make you free.

This book will require consistent effort on your part. But you can do it. The Holy Spirit is effectually working in you, energizing and creating in you the power and desire both to will and to work for His good pleasure. God has given you a spirit of discipline. You can do it.

I believe that if you were to dedicate one hour a day to immerse yourself in the pages of this book, and continually apply what you learn in every area of your life, you *will* be positively affected. And your effectiveness as a Christian *will* significantly increase.

My prayer is that God will use this book to have His best fulfilled in your life. Go for it!

—Pastor Ian M. Taylor
Ian Taylor Ministries Inc.
Hamilton, Ontario, Canada

Section I

Insightful Biblical Truths

"Open my eyes, that I may see wondrous things from Your law." (Psalm 119:18)

The Majesty of God's Word

"In the beginning was the word and the word was with God, and the word was God."
-John 1:1

The Word is God. God and His Word are one. The Word is as God is. The Word is alive. The Word is a discerner of your thoughts, motives, and intents of your heart (Hebrews 4:12).The way you treat and approach the Word, will determine the way the Word treats you. Everything and everyone is naked and open to the eyes of the Word. (Hebrews 4:13). The way you measure the Word, will determine the way the grace of God is measured back to you (Mark 4:24). The Word says: I love them that love me, (Proverbs 8:17) and whosoever despises me (thinks little of me) and my counsel, brings destruction upon himself. But he who reverences and respects me is rewarded (Proverbs 13:13). Jesus said anyone (sinner or saint) who rejects me and my Word, the Word shall judge him on the last day (John 12:48).

Great is the mystery of Godliness. God was manifest in the flesh (1 Timothy 3:16). "The Word was made flesh" (John 1:14). Some spiritual things are hard to understand, nevertheless, you receive them by faith and choose to believe them. God and His Word are one. Your attitude and reverence for God's Word is your reverence for God. The Word is as majestic, powerful, and holy as God is. Your heart needs to stand in awe of the Word. You are to have the same attitude as God has towards His own Word. You are to magnify God's Word even above His name (Psalm 138:2).

Section I - Insightful Biblical Truths

WARNING! Do not let the Bible be just like any other book.

Think on These Things

1. The Word is the Father speaking to you.

2. The Word is personal.

3. God is love (I John 4:8) and God is the Word (John 1:1) therefore the Word is love.

4. The Word is love affectionately looking into your eyes and saying I love you with an everlasting love, I am covenanted to you and I will never leave you nor forsake you (Hebrews 13:5). Never fear for I am God, your God. I will help you and strengthen you. I will hold you up with my victorious right hand (Isaiah 41:10). I am your rock, your refuge, your defense, and your salvation. I am all you could ever need and I am devoted to you. Trust me at all times. Pour out your heart before me. I will heal you and comfort you (Psalm 62:5-8). I am your shepherd, you shall not want. Just let me be your Lord (Psalm 23:1). I will supply all your need according to my riches (Philippians 4:19). Don't let circumstances and man's limitations control your reasoning and strangle your faith (2 Corinthians 10:5). Have the mind of Christ (1 Corinthians 2:16). Come let us reason together (Isaiah 1:18). All things are possible with me (Matthew 19:26). And you are with me so all things are possible to you, if you would only believe (Mark 9:23). Humbly submit to me and let your hope and expectation be from me (Psalm 62:5). I am Love, I am God, and I am the Word! The Word is love's voice talking to you.

The Word, the Word, the Word

1. Takes the place of Jesus delivering a message to you from the Father.
2. The Word is Christ Himself revealed.
3. The Word is the mind of God and the will of God.
4. The Word has the authority of God (Psalm 107:20).
5. The Word has creative and re-creative power.
6. You are born again of the Word (1 Peter 1:23).
7. The Word has healing power for the sick (Psalm 107:20).
8. The Word has deliverance for the oppressed.
9. The Word has hope for the discouraged.
10. The Word has strength for the weak.
11. The Word has life for the dead.

The Word is bread from Heaven. You are to esteem the Word coming out of God's mouth more highly than your necessary food (Job 23:12).

1. God is jealous over His Word and—watches over His word to perform it (Jeremiah 1:12).
2. If you want to be upheld and come through the storms of life victoriously, you must stand on the Word for He upholds all things by the Word of His power (Hebrews 1:3).
3. If you obey the Word, the Word will obey you (John 14:21; John 15:7).

Will you allow the Word to govern you and take the place as master in your life?

Let the Word be the final authority in your life. Align your thoughts, your mind and your actions to agree with God's Word.

The Word is Your Life
(Deuteronomy 32:47)

God is not only in His Word and backs up His Word but flows out of His Word as the Word comes out of your mouth. The Bible teaches that through meditation and acting on the Word, you are to let the Word of God dwell in you richly (Colossians 3:16) and let it flow out of your lips. When you present to men the Word of God, you are literally imparting into their hearts a living thing that God can use to change their lives (Philippians 2:16).

The Word is able to build you up, give you grace, reveal your inheritance (Acts 20:32), and build faith into your heart (Romans 10:14) so you can possess your inheritance. The Word of God educates your mind and spirit about righteousness, your authority, the name of Jesus, the promises of God and spiritual things (2 Timothy 3: 16, 17 and 1 Corinthians 12 :1). The Word is truth that sanctifies you, and sets you apart for the fellowship and service of God (John 17:17; Ephesians 5:26). The Word of God will mold and shape your character to be conformed to Christ's character (Colossians 1:28; Romans 8:29; 2 Timothy 3:16,17).The Word of God renews your mind so you can walk in agreement with God (Romans 12:2; Ephesians 4:18; Amos 3:3).

What is the conclusion of the whole matter? Let the Word of God dwell in you richly, for it is your life. You can be a 'Psalm 112 saint of God'.

The Absolute Importance of Your Confession

Remember God's Word is the absolute truth and one hundred percent accurate. Consider the following versus of scripture as we join and loop them together. *"A man's belly shall be satisfied with the fruit of his mouth, and with the consequences of his mouth he must be satisfied"* (Proverbs 18:20). *"Death and life are in the power of the tongue and they who indulge it shall eat the fruit of it"* (for death or for life) (Proverbs 18:21). Words go down into the innermost parts of the belly (Proverbs 18:8) and as the scripture says, from his innermost being shall flow continuously springs and rivers of living (or dead) water (John 7:38). My tongue is like the pen of a ready writer (Psalms 45:1) writing upon the tablet of my heart, my innermost parts, (Proverbs 3:3). Now I must keep and guard my heart with all diligence and vigilance, above all that I guard for out of it flows the springs (or forces) of life (Proverbs 4:23). Therefore I must give the devil no place (Ephesians 4:27) and let no corrupt (unbelieving) communication proceed out of my mouth; but only what is good and beneficial (Ephesians 4:27 personal paraphrase). According to James 3:2, if I do not offend in speech (never say the wrong things) I am a fully developed character and perfect man, able to control my whole body and to curb my entire nature.

Here is the Conclusion

The words that come out of my mouth (Matthew 12:34) will program my heart which will release forces of life or death which will control my attitude, thoughts, emotions, actions, and in turn my destiny (Matthew 15:19).

Here is the Truth

You will have the things you say and believe in your heart (Mark 11:23). *"For with the heart man believes and with the mouth confession is made unto..."* For better or worst, you are the prophet of your life. "By your words you shall be justified or condemned" (Matthew 12:37).

If you took time to study and meditate on the above verses you will come to understand how and why "Confession of your Faith" works (Hebrews 10:23). Now let's consider the implication of your confessions (the continual stream of words that proceed from your lips). What impact do they truly have on your life?

1. **Salvation** – Comes from the Greek word *soteria* which means more than being saved; it includes deliverance, preservation, soundness, prosperity, happiness, rescue, and general well being.

Romans 10:10 says: *"with the mouth confession is made unto salvation"* (wholeness, happiness, prosperity, deliverance etc).

Psalm 70:4 instructs that if you love God's salvation you should say (confess) continually *'let God be magnified.'* So your confession is directly linked to your great salvation.

2. **Angelic Protection** – Hebrews 1:14 tells us that angels are ministering spirits sent out in the service of God for the assistance of those who are to inherit salvation (this includes you and me and all who are children of God). Psalm 103:20 says: *"the angels excel in strength and do God's commandments and harken to the voice of His word."* You and I do not own angels, however they are assigned to assist us and to help fulfill God's commandments and Word in *our* lives. They are activated and commissioned when we give voice to God's Word in faith and love. It would help our understanding to see them as waiters in

God's restaurant assigned to your table to serve you. But you must place your order verbally based on God's menu which is His Word and promises. Observe in Daniel 10:12, when the angel appeared to Daniel, he said: *"your words were heard and I am come because of your words."* Your words move and affect the activity of angels.

3. **Divine Protection and Deliverance** – Psalm 91 is a great psalm promising divine protection, deliverance, and long life. These are some conditions that position you for the benefits of Psalm 91. Psalm 91 will work for you because:

   a. you have made the Lord your refuge and dwelling place (v. 9)

   b. you have set your love upon God (v. 14), and

   c. you know God's Name (v. 14).

   Notice how Psalm 91:2 emphasizes that you should *say (confess)* that the Lord is your refuge and fortress and your God, and that you do trust Him. *So Psalm 91 is yours as you claim it with your mouth, believe it in your heart, and have the right corresponding actions.*

4. **Devils & Demons** – The Spirit of God, Who is the Spirit of Truth and perfect understanding states in 1 Corinthians 10:10 that the children of Israel were *"destroyed by the destroyer because of their murmuring."* The psalmist David said that by keeping God's Word in his mouth he was kept from the paths of the destroyer (Psalm 17:4) and he was therefore determined that he

should not transgress with his mouth (Psalm 17:3). We are exhorted in Philippians 2:14-15 to do all things without murmuring and complaining so that we might be blameless and harmless, manifested as the sons of God in the midst of a wicked and crooked generation. We are not to be ignorant concerning the implication of our words and confessions, as most non-Christians are. Sometimes carnal babes in Christ who are controlled by their senses, and reasoning and not by the truth of God's Word are also ignorant concerning the power of their words/confessions. You must not walk and talk according to the vanity of the unrenewed mind (Ephesians 4:17). But rather, our speech must always be with grace seasoned with the Word (Colossians 4:6), so that we might give no place to the devil (Ephesians 4:27). But let's do as James instructed. *"Resist the devil and he will flee from you"* (James 4:7). How? Like Jesus did when He was tempted in the wilderness. He used the Word to resist the devil, when He said: *"It is written"* (Matthew 4:4,7,10).

5. **God the Holy Spirit** – According to Galatians 3:5, the Holy Spirit who is the member of the God-head that performs miracles in our lives, does it, not based on the works of the law but by "the hearing of faith". When the Holy Spirit hears faith filled words proceeding from your heart and mouth, He performs miracles. It is not by your might nor by your power but by the Holy Spirit (Zechariah 4:6) that miracles are performed. But the Holy Spirit must hear *your* faith. James said: *"faith without works is dead"* (James 2:20). The Spirit of faith believes according to the Word of God and thusly speaks (2 Corinthians 4:13). Faith must have a voice.

6. **Jesus our High Priest** – Hebrews 3:1 says: *"Wherefore*

Holy brethren, partakers of the heavenly calling, consider (thoughtfully and attentively) the Apostle and High priest of our profession; Christ Jesus." The same Greek word that translates 'profession' here, is translated elsewhere in the King James Version as 'confession'. Many modern Bible translations use the word 'confession'. When we read this meaning into Hebrews 3:1, we conclude that Jesus Christ has been sent (Apostle means 'sent one') and appointed by God the Father to stand in the office of High Priest over our confessions (these are the declarations of our lips that agree with God's Word). Hebrews 4:14 instructs, "seeing then that we have a great High Priest, that is passed into the heavens, Jesus the Son of God, let us hold fast our confession." Hebrews 10:23 adds: *"Hold fast the confession of our faith without wavering."*

So then, your confession gives Jesus something to work with as He represents you, as your Apostle and High priest, at the right hand of the Father.

Did not Jesus say in Matthew 10:32 that if you confess Him before men He will confess you before the Father? Well, to confess Jesus before men, you must confess the Word since Jesus and His Word are one and the same.

Your confession is important to the angels of God, the devil, and his demons. The mighty Holy Spirit, and Jesus your High Priest, and God your Heavenly Father. Your prayer and determined purpose ought to be *"Let the words of my mouth and the meditation of my heart be acceptable in Your sight and presence O God"* (Psalm 19:14).

7. **Poverty or Riches** – Proverbs 16:15 says, *"the destruction of the poor is their poverty",* and Proverbs

18:7 says, *"a fool's mouth is his destruction."* Combining these scriptures, we conclude that one's mouth can chart a course leading to his destruction and ruin. Let me put it another way. The poor man's poverty is enforced by his mouth and speech. Life and death is in the power of the tongue (Proverbs 18:21). You can talk your way out of poverty and into prosperity. Jesus said you can have what you say if you believe it in your heart and say it continually with your mouth (Mark 11:23).

The poor man stays poor because he keeps saying what he sees and has in the physical, based on his senses, reasoning and knowledge, instead of what he desires—prosperity and increase. This is how things are in the Spirit and in the Kingdom of God (Ephesians 1:3,11; Luke 17:21,2; Corinthians 8:9).

Proverbs 13:2 says, *"a man shall eat good by the fruit of his mouth."* God told Joshua do not let the Word of God depart from your mouth but keep saying it and meditate in it and you will make your own way prosperous and have good success (Joshua 1:8).

So you are not to remain captive by circumstances and your environment. God has given you authority-the Word is near you, even in your mouth and in your heart (Romans 10:8). You have the blessing of the Lord in Christ (Galatians 3:14, 29), and the blessing of the Lord will make you rich without sorrow coming with it (Proverbs 10:22). So put your mouth to work, begin to prosper as your soul prospers (3 John 2), and give God your Father delight and joy (Psalm 35:27) since He delights in your prosperity and then you will walk and live out the truth of the Gospel (2 John 4). Good news! You do not have to be poor any more.

Confession is not the only principle involved in your prosperity but it is of major importance.

8. **Your Faith** – In Luke 17:5 Jesus' apostles asked Him how to increase their faith. Jesus answered by saying (and I paraphrase), faith is like a mustard seed you need to plant it by saying and speaking, and second you need to exercise constantly by putting your faith to work by saying to the 'sycamore trees' in your life what it is you desire. Study this portion of scripture—Luke 17:5-10. Jesus speaks of faith as your servant given to you by God as a gift (Romans 12:3) to help you possess the things that are promised to you in Christ. And without faith it is impossible to please God. Faith is what causes you to possess the victories that are yours in Christ (1 John 5:4). How does faith work? Faith works by words, and by your confession. Romans 4:17 says, faith "calls those things which be not as though they were." Faith confesses and makes declarations. Second Corinthians 4:13 says, the Spirit of faith believes and speaks accordingly. So then faith must have a voice. Your voice and your confession. Confession is a necessary ingredient to build your faith, increase your faith, exercise your faith, and release your faith.

God's Word contains the faith of God, and Romans 10:8 calls it the Word of faith. Faith comes and is deposited in your heart from God's Word when you keep saying and confessing, and your physical and spiritual ears keep hearing the faith-filled words of God.

Conclusion: faith is deposited in your heart by you confessing God's Word consistently and continually.

Fear which is the opposite of faith can also build up in your heart by confessing the devil's fear filled, unbelieving, negative words of defeat, failure, and death.

Choose life, choose to confess God's Word, victory, success and strength.

So then confessions are of absolute importance to your faith, and to its development and deployment.

9. **Your Thoughts** – Negative, unbelieving thoughts will come to your mind. If you confess those thoughts you will be taking those thoughts and making them your own. Jesus warned, do not take any anxious or wrong thoughts by saying them (Matthew 6:31). You can choose to stop any negative thought by speaking the positive powerful Word of God. It is called bringing every thought captive and making it obey Christ, according to 2 Corinthians 10:5.

10. **Your Emotions** – Proverbs 15:23 says that a man has joy by the answer of his mouth. When you confess your confident expectation of victory based on God's Word and promises, and rejoice before God, it is very difficult to feel oppressed, beaten down, and sad. The way you talk will affect the way you think. And the way you think will affect the way you feel. The truth is, a glad heart has a continual feast, regardless of the circumstances (Proverbs 15:15).

    Confessing God's Word programs your heart, renews your mind, affects your thinking, and influences your feelings and emotions.

11. **Your health** — Proverbs 16:24 declares that *"pleasant words are as a honey comb, sweet to the soul and health*

to the bones." Speaking the right words bring joy to the heart (Proverbs 15:23). And a merry heart is like medicine (Proverbs 17:22). A gentle tongue (with its healing power) is a tree of life. On the other hand, a willful contrariness in the tongue breaks down the spirit (Proverbs 15:4 Amplified), and a broken spirit dries up the bones (Proverbs 17:22).

A calm and undisturbed mind and heart are the life and health of the body, but envy, jealousy, and wrath are like rottenness of the bones (Proverbs 14:30 Amplified). The Word of God is health to all your flesh (Proverbs 4:22). Speaking and confessing God's Word is part of the process of getting the Word into your heart so its healing power can flow out to your bones, organs, and your whole being (Psalm 107:20).

Your divine health is in your mouth. Life and death is in the power of your tongue—choose life (Proverbs 18:21).

Final Conclusion:

Your confession affects every area of your life: Your thoughts, your attitudes, your emotions, your actions, your will, your health, your prosperity, your salvation, your deliverance, the activity of the angels in your life, your authority over devils and demons, your faith, your divine protection, the renewing and reprogramming of your mind, your meditation in God's Word, the miracle working power of the Holy Spirit, the High Priest ministry of Christ and your destiny.

Job 22:28 says that you shall also decide and decree a thing and it shall be established for you and the light of God's favour shall shine upon your ways. So truly your life is affected by your confession.

Through reading this book, you will be encouraged to come up higher in your confessions and become a master of your confession. God has given you authority and dominion. Use it for the glory of God and His Kingdom.

Biblical Meditation
The Master Key for Success

"Blessed (prosperous; having supernatural power working for him) is the man who walks and lives not in the counsel of the ungodly (following their advice, their plans and purposes)... but delight in the law of the Lord (God's Word) and in His law (God's law, teachings and instructions) he habitually meditates (ponders and studies) by day and by night. He shall be like a tree firmly planted by the streams of water, ready to bring forth its fruit in its season, its leaf shall not wither and everything he does shall prosper" (Psalm 1:1-3).

"This book of the law (God's Word) shall not depart out of your mouth (do not say anything that does not agree with God's Word). But you shall meditate (ponder, study and delight yourself in) God's Word day and night, (habitually) that you may observe and do according to all that is written in it. For then you shall make your way prosperous, deal wisely and have good success" (Joshua 1:8).

"Delight yourself in the Lord and He will give you the desires of your heart" (Psalm 37:4). *"If you abide in Me and my words abide in you, and you shall ask what you will and it shall be done for you"* (John 15:7). In other words, if you delight yourself in the Lord and let His Words be your delight, so that they are engrafted and embedded in your heart and

life, you shall ask what you will and have the experience of having all your prayers answered. That is success and prosperity!

Now all four of these references of God's Word are talking about 'Biblical Meditation' that produces a blessed and prosperous life. To be blessed is to have God's supernatural power working for you. True prosperity is having the ability to use God's power to meet your own needs, and the needs of mankind, in all areas of life.

Now the Word of God is the power of God. The Word has creative and recreative power. The Word is able to do all that God can do. All things are naked and defenseless to the Word. The Word of God is the power of God unto salvation, wholeness, deliverance, prosperity, divine health and protection. The Word of God is unlimited in power and wisdom (Romans 1:16; Hebrews 1:3; Hebrews 11:3; Hebrews 4:13; 1 Corinthians 1:18). Biblical meditation is a divine process that God has given to you and me, by which you interact and become intimate with His Word. This will release the wisdom, power, and life that is in God's Word, into your life.

Biblical meditation is a process by which the eternal, timeless Word of God becomes engrafted and embedded in your heart, renews your mind and restores your soul (James 1:21; Romans 12:2; Psalm 23:2). There are several keys and principles that will affect your prosperity; they are all important: Prayer (2 Chronicles 26:5), faith (1 John 5:4), confession (Matthew 17:20), love (1 Corinthians 13:8), the fear of the Lord and humility (Proverbs 22:4). However, consider the following thoughts:

41

The apostles said, *"We will devote and exercise ourselves continually to prayer and to the ministry of the Word"* (Acts 6:4). The Word has a ministry to perform in your life. The Word will perform and accomplish its assignment in your life if given the opportunity. Remember, no Word from God is without power and is impossible of fulfillment (Luke 1:37).

Here is a provoking question: What if the Word of God is allowed to have free course in your heart and life and is permitted by your will, choices, cooperation and discipline to fulfill its ministry in you and through you? Would God's perfect will be accomplished in your life? Would you be totally successful and prosperous by Heaven's standards? I believe without a doubt the answer is: yes, yes, yes, and amen!

Meditation is your intimate, reverential interaction with God's Word that will cause God's Word to be engrafted in your life and have dominion and Lordship over you and in you. In other words, biblical meditation will cause the Word of God to have free course in your life and fulfill its ministry in you. The meditation process will enlarge your heart so that you will become willing and will obey His commandments (Psalm 119:32). You will become a doer of the Word and not a hearer only (James 1:22). The Word teaches you to exercise and develop in the other keys and principles of success such as prayer, walking in faith that works by love, walking in the Spirit, humility, the fear of the Lord, and holiness. ***Again, let me emphasize, biblical meditation is not the only key, but it is God's master key for your total success for every area of your life.***

- ***To delight involves your emotions.***

    What does the Bible tell us about meditating? Psalm 1:2

says, *"but his delight is in God's Word and in God's Word he meditates day and night".* So then, to meditate in God's Word is to delight yourself in the Word. By definition, *"to delight"* means to desire, have pleasure, favour, to enjoy.

- **To meditate involves your attitude.**

Psalm 119:15 says, *"I will meditate in Your precepts and have respect to Your ways."* So then, to meditate in the Word is to have respect and high regard for God's Word.

- **To meditate involves your memory.**

Psalm 119:16 says, *"I will delight myself in Your statutes, I will not forget Your Word."* So then, to meditate in God's Word includes remembering the Word.

- **To meditate in God's Word is to love God's Word.**

Psalm 119:107 says: *"I will delight myself in your commandments which I have loved."* In addition, according to John 14:21 to love God's Word is to be committed and obedient to the Word. Meditating on God's Word involves your heart and your will.

- **To meditate in God's Word involves your mouth.**

Joshua 1:8 says, *"This book of the law shall not depart from your mouth, but you shall meditate therein day and night."* Therefore, to meditate in God's Word involves keeping God's Word in your mouth by confirming and muttering it.

- **To meditate is to imagine.**

  Psalm 2:1 says, *"Why do the heathen rage, and the people imagine a vain thing?"* In the Greek, the word *'imagine'* is also translated here as *'meditate'*.

- **To meditate in God's Word involves your soul.**

  It is no surprise James 1:21 says: *"receive with meekness the engrafted word, which is able to save your soul."* Again, in Psalm 19:7 it says, *"the Word of God is perfect converting the soul."*

- **Meditating includes pondering over the Word of God and rejoicing over the Word.**

  Psalm 63:5,6 says: *"My mouth shall praise thee with joyful lips, when I remember you upon my bed and meditate on you in the night watches."*

Proverbs 4:20-24 and Deuteronomy 11:18-21 describes the process of meditating. To meditate in the Word is to mutter, confess audibly, study, rejoice over, memorize, keep before your eyes, keep it coming into your ear (by listening), visualizing (by imagining), obeying (by acting on) and pondering the Word of God constantly. Meditating is immersing yourself in the Word. Paul told Timothy: "Meditate on these things, give yourself wholly to them." When you meditate on God's Word you must also abide in it (John 15:7). It is no surprise that as you correctly meditate in God's Word these things will follow: you will have days of Heaven on earth (Deuteronomy 11:21); whatever you do will prosper (Psalm 1:3); your profiting and prosperity will be evident to everyone (1 Timothy 4:15); the desires of your heart will come from God (Philippians 2:13) and be fulfilled (Psalm 37:4).

Biblical Meditation:

1. **Will deliver you from sin.** Psalm 119:11: *"Thy word have I hid in my heart, that I might not sin against you."*
2. **Will break the power of every addiction in your life.** John 8:31, 32: *"if you continue in the word... you will know the truth and the truth will set you free".* James 1:25 calls the Word the perfect law of liberty.
3. **Will produce purity in your life.** Psalm 119:9: *"How shall a young man cleanse his ways? By taking heed according to God's Word."*
4. **Will fix and align your heart to the Word.** (Matthew 15:18, 19 and Colossians 3:16).
5. **Will renew your mind.** (Romans 12:2).
6. **Will produce prosperity** (3 John 2).
7. **Will produce wisdom and prosperity** (Proverbs 3:13, 14).
8. **Will open the door to revelation knowledge.** Psalm 119:99 says: *"I have more understanding than all my teachers, because your words are my meditation."*

- *Meditation* produces Revelation.
- *Revelation* produces Motivation.
- *Motivation* produces Action.
- *Action* produces Manifestation.
- *Manifestation* produces **Victory and Success.**

Finally, how do you meditate?

1. Interact with the Word in every way possible

2. Read the Word
3. Study the Word
4. Listen to the Word preached (listen to tapes and CDs constantly)
5. Memorize the Word
6. Write the Word down on cards and post it somewhere where you will constantly see it
7. Make notes when you study
8. Sing the Word
9. Visualize the Word fulfilled
10. Read the same verse in different translations
11. Confess the Word
12. Mutter the Word
13. Pray the Word
14. Understand the Word
15. Pray in the Spirit by praying in other tongues (1 Corinthians 15:2,4)

Proverbs 6:21, 22 says, when you meditate on the Word continually wherever you go, the Word will lead you and guide you. When you sleep, It shall keep you (you may even dream about the Word), when you awake It will speak to you.

My dear fellow saint, when you begin, the Word will be as a small mustard seed, but as you meditate in it continually, it will become as a huge tree of righteousness in your heart and life and will be a blessing to both you and others (Matthew 13:31, 32 and Isaiah 61:3). Allow me to share with you a few things that will help you meditate on the Word: You will not meditate continually if you do not first make a decision; second, have a plan; and third, police yourself. Begin today! Let the Holy Spirit direct you to verses for you to meditate in.

Now, go for it in Jesus' name!

I encourage you to immerse yourself in the pages of this book for one hour daily. You will be blessed.

Provoking Thoughts on Prayer

1. To fail to pray is preparing to fail.

2. He who does not pray, robs himself of God's help.

3. Prayer seeks God.

4. To not pray is to leave God out of the equation of your everyday life.

5. Prayerlessness is pride. To not pray is to say, "God I can handle this on my own." Humility says, "I can of myself do nothing, (John 15:5) Lord you are my sufficiency" (2 Corinthians 3:5).

6. Prayer is an affirmation of your dependency on God.

7. According to 1 Samuel 12:23, prayerlessness is sin.

8. Prayer opens the door for God to be involved in your life. James 4:2 says, *"You have not, because you ask not."*

9. According to Isaiah 30:18 the Lord earnestly waits expecting, looking, and longing to be gracious to those that are earnestly waiting for Him. God delights in showing Himself strong on behalf of those that trust Him, love Him, seek Him, and obey Him (2 Chronicles 16:9).

10. According to Isaiah 64:4 God works and shows Himself active on behalf of them that earnestly wait for Him.

11. God says He loves and is covenant-committed to them who love Him. And those that seek Him early shall find Him. Remember, riches and honour are with Him. And he leads in the way that is right and just. He Will cause those who love Him to inherit true riches, and will fill their treasures (Proverbs 8:21). The Lord will teach you how to profit, and lead you in the way you should go (Isaiah 48:17).

12. As long as you seek the Lord He will make you prosper (2 Chronicles 26:5).

13. Prayer puts you into the holy presence of God Almighty. Prayer ushers you into the throne room through the blood of Christ (Hebrews 10:19).

14. In His presence, He will show you the path of life (Psalm 16:11). In His presence He will show you great and mighty things which you do not know (Jeremiah 33:3).

15. In His presence, He will teach you, instruct you, and give you revelation knowledge and understanding (Psalm 73:17).

16. In His presence, He will place desires, visions and dreams in your heart (Philippians 2:13).

17. In His presence, He will transform you, mold you, and fill you with His love and compassion.

18. They that wait on the Lord shall renew their strength (Isaiah 40:31). In His presence, He will empower you, energize you and establish you.

19. In His presence He will fill you with Himself.

20. Prayer is a closet in which intimacy with God is developed.

21. Prayer is the place where you become sensitive to the heart and voice of God.

22. Prayer is the birth chamber where visions, dreams and God-ideas are born.

23. Prayer is the crucible in which we are refined to be God's 'battle axe' (Jeremiah 51:20).

24. Prayer is partnering with Heaven for the will of God to be done on earth (Matthew 18:18-20).

25. Prayer gives God the legal right to move in our lives, family, church and in the earth (2 Chronicles 7:14, Ezekiel 22:30).

26. Prayer causes spiritual power that changes things to be released in our lives and in the earth (James 5:16).

27. Prayer opens doors for the gospel to prosper in the hearts of men (2 Thessalonians 3:1).

28. Prayer empowers the witness of Gospel (Ephesians 6:18,19).

29. Prayer causes a supply of the anointing by the Spirit of God (Philippians 1:19).

30. The apostles of the early church said: "We will devote

ourselves continually to prayer, and to the ministry of the Word" (Acts 6:4).

31. You can preach and share divine truths that are not energized by the Spirit of God due to lack of prayer. Jesus, a man of prayer said: *"The words that I speak unto you are of spirit and of life"* (John 6:63).

32. A prayer-filled life will empower your words to impact the hearts of men (1 Corinthians 2:4).

33. It is impossible for a believer to stay in harmony with God's will for his life, without a lifestyle of prayer.

34. God is able to work effectively through you to the degree that you give yourself to prayer and to the Word.

35. Satan effectively disarms you when he keeps you too busy to stop and pray.

36. You must not be seduced in being satisfied with doing what is good, while neglecting what is best: the word and prayer (Luke 10:42).

37. When you, I and the church fail to pray, decay and evil will prevail (2 Chronicles 7:14).

Prayer is part of your faith life. Prayer seeks God, believing that *"He is and that He is a rewarder of those that diligently seek Him"* (Hebrews 11:6). Let's consider the parable that Jesus told in Luke 18:1-8, regarding the widow who came to the unjust judge demanding justice. The parable is about prayer, yet Jesus asked the question in verse 8: *"When the Son of Man comes, shall He find faith on the earth?"* Jesus connected faith with your prayer life. In other words, Jesus asked, when He returned, will He find men believing and diligently seeking God? Or would prayerlessness be rampant?

The Bible warns that, *"in the latter days some will depart from the faith, giving heed to seducing spirits, and doctrines of devils"* (1 Timothy 4:1). We are living in an age when "the god of self-help" is enthroned in our society and seeks to enter the churches. First John 2:16, according to the Amplified Bible, describes the *'pride of life'* as being an assurance in one's own resources, or in the stability of earthly things and adds that these do not come from the Father God, but from the world itself. We must continually wait upon God and let our expectation be from Him (Psalm 62:5).

It is important that you develop a daily prayer life. Here are **seven keys to help you develop a constant prayer life:**

1. Make a decision to pray everyday. If possible, in a specific location at a specific time.
2. Make confessions about your prayer life. You may use some of the confessions in this book.
3. Meditate on a few particular scriptures that speak to you, such as Mark 1:35.
4. Read Word-based books on prayer continually.
5. Get involved in prayer groups in your church. Remember the spirit of prayer can be contagious.
6. Stay in fellowship with God all day long. Continue to practice the presence of God.
7. There are times you may not feel like praying; however you are not to walk by feelings. According to Isaiah 64:7, you need to stir yourself up to pray.

Total Identification:
Based on the Perfect Substitutionary Works of Christ

Romans 8:17 says: we are to share Christ's suffering if we are to share His glory. In other words, we must totally identify with Jesus' death, burial, resurrection and ascension if we are to live in the reality of His resurrection. Romans 6:3-5 says: *"Know ye not, that so many of us as were baptized into Jesus Christ were baptized into his death? Therefore we are buried with him by baptism into death: that like as Christ was raised up from the dead by the glory of the Father, even so we also should walk in newness of life. For if we have been planted together in the likeness of his death, we shall be also in the likeness of his resurrection."*

Jesus' perfect work of substitution on our behalf is the basis of Redemption and gives us the legal right to our authority in Christ over hell, death, the grave, sin, sickness, and poverty. "Christ has redeemed us from the curse of the law, being made a curse for us. For it is written, cursed is everyone that hangs on a tree" (Galatians 3:13).

Here is a summary of our identification with Christ's substitutionary work on our behalf:

A. Galatians 2:20 – We **were crucified** with Christ.
B. Romans 6:8 – We **have died** with Christ.
C. Colossians 2:12 – We **were buried** with Christ
D. First Timothy 3:16, Romans 4:25, and 2 Corinthians 5:21, together reveal that Jesus was made sin with our sin, betrayed and put to death because of our offenses, and raised up again after He was justified in the Spirit and we **are justified with** Him.
E. Colossians 12:13 – we **were made alive** together with Him.
F. Ephesians 2:6 – we **were raised up** together with Him, and made to **sit together** with Him in heavenly places at the right hand of the Majesty on High (Hebrews 1:3).

This is the scriptural picture of your identification with Christ and therefore, *"As He is, so are you in this world"* (1John 4:17).

The Power of Thanksgiving

The ability to choose to give God thanks is a tremendous gift of grace given to you as a child of God. The giving of thanks always will connect you with the will of God for your life, while setting you apart for the Lord, protecting your heart from the contaminating fiery darts of the wicked, insulating you from the enemy and establishing you in faith. Giving thanks unto the Lord will cause you to be triumphant and victorious over your enemies (2 Corinthians 2:14; Psalms 8:2).

Let us examine the Word and make some observations regarding thanksgiving.

- First Thessalonians 5:18: *"Thank God in everything no matter what the circumstances may be. Be thankful and give thanks for this is the will of God for you",* who are in Christ Jesus, who is the revealer and mediator of the will of God.

- Thanksgiving connects you to the will of God for your life. First Thessalonians 4:3 (amplified): this is the will of God, that you should be consecrated (separated and set apart for pure and holy living, living as unto the Lord).

- Thanksgiving, which is God's will for you at all times will set you apart from the spirit of the world and consecrate you to the Lord. Philippians 2:14, 15 (amplified) do all things without grumbling, fault-finding and complaining... that you may show yourself to be blameless and guileless, innocent, and an uncontaminated child of God without blemish in the midst of a crooked and wicked generation (spiritually perverted and perverse) among whom you are sent as a bright light in the world.

* Thankfulness protects your attitude and your heart from bitterness, resentment, pride, murmuring, etc (Proverbs 4;23; Hebrews 12:15).

* Your thankful attitude gives you a fragrance distinct from the unthankful spirit that is in the world (2 Timothy 3:2).

* Thankfulness connects you with the light of the "Zoë" life of God (Philippians 2:15, John 1:4, John 8:12) and makes your life an epistle of Christ (2 Corinthians 3:3). You become a more effective witness (2 Corinthians 4:4, 6). Do not fret or have anxiety about anything, but in every circumstance and in everything, by prayer and petition (define requests) with thanksgiving continue to make your 'wants' known to God (Philippians 4:6).

* Thanksgiving releases the force of faith in your prayers and daily walk. Psalms 50:23: He who brings an offering of praise and thanksgiving honours and glorifies the Lord, and he who orders his conduct (his behavior, speech and attitude) aright, to him the Lord will demonstrate His salvation, deliverance, protection and provisions.

* Your thanksgiving honours God.

- Your thanksgiving affects your conduct.

- Your thanksgiving opens the door for God to demonstrate His Salvation. Therefore, at all times, offer up to God a sacrifice of praise which is the fruit of your lips giving thanks to His name (Hebrews 13:15).

- Thanksgiving is an aspect of praise, and God has ordained praise as a means to silence the enemy (Psalm 8:2).

Conclusion: What should our response be to these truths regarding thanksgiving? Our response should be the decision that says: "I will give thanks to the Lord always in all things, for this is God's will for me and because my thanksgiving honours and blesses God my Lord."

The Power of Rejoicing

"Rejoice in the Lord always (delight yourself in Him) and again I say Rejoice!" (Philippians 4:4). God did not request that you do something that you are incapable of doing. You can do all things through Christ who makes you able (Philippians 4:13). You choose to rejoice in the Lord, not in the circumstances. You make a quality decision to rejoice inspite of the circumstances. Why is this so important? Here are some reasons:

1. The Bible says in Psalm 33:1: *"Rejoice in the Lord O ye who are righteous, for praise is appropriate for those who are upright in heart."*

2. Rejoicing is a part of how you release and express praise

to the Lord. As appropriate as it is for birds to fly, even so it is appropriate for the redeemed of the Lord to rejoice in the Lord and praise Him.

3. All reasons for which you should praise the Lord are also reasons why you should rejoice in the Lord.

When you praise God you enthrone Him in your life and circumstances (Psalm 22:3). In 2 Chronicles 20:22, when the children of Israel praised the Lord, God set ambushes against their enemies. When you praise and rejoice before the Lord He will arise and your enemies will be scattered (Psalm 68:1). So God has ordained praise to be a weapon against your foes (Psalm 8:2).

To rejoice means to return to the source of your joy and to be refilled with Joy. Guess what? The joy of the Lord is your strength (Nehemiah 8:10). As you rejoice, the Lord will help you and strengthen you (Isaiah 41:10, Isaiah 40:31). Rejoicing and praising the Lord is ministering and waiting on the Lord. As you wait on the Lord, the Lord will refresh and rejuvenate you (Acts 3:19).

Rejoicing in the Lord will hook you up to the anointing and power of God (Isaiah 61:1,3). Rejoicing in the Lord will enable you to draw whatever grace and sufficiency you need from the wells of God's salvation (Isaiah 12:3). Rejoice in the Lord always and He will protect your joy in the midst of battle (James 1:2); and release spiritual power to gird up the loins of your mind (1 Peter 1:8,13) while protecting your heart from the devices of Satan (Proverbs 4:23, 2 Corinthians 2:11).

Joy is also a force that you can use in prayer. Paul said he makes requests with joy (Philippians 1:4; 1 Thessalonians 3:9). You can scare the devil off by rejoicing. Philippians

1:28 says, "Do not for a moment be frightened or intimidated in anything by your adversaries. For such constancy and fearlessness will be a sign to them of their impending destruction but a token of your deliverance and salvation from God."

Now you may say "Sometimes I feel so beaten down, discouraged and weak to resist the devil, much less fight." Let me say to you, first of all, you must walk by faith not by your feelings. Second, your fight is the fight of faith (1 Timothy 6:12). In First Peter 5:8-9, the Bible says: "Be sober, be vigilant; because your adversary the devil, as a roaring lion, walks about, seeking whom he may devour: Whom resist steadfast in the faith." Here is some understanding that will help you: To rejoice means to return to the source of your joy. If your car is out of gas, what should you do? Go to the gas station and fill up. So if your joy level is low, go to the source of your joy and refill.

What is the source of your joy? In His presence is fullness of joy (Psalm 16:11). So get into His presence and let the spirit of God refill you. Enter His presence by mixing faith with the Blood of Christ (Hebrews 10:19). Spend time in prayer. If you are able to pray in tongues, spend some time praying in tongues. Obey Psalm 100: *"make a joyful noise, enter His gates with thanksgiving, and His courts with praise."*

Joy is a fruit of the Holy Spirit (Galatians 5:22; Romans 14:17; Luke 17:21). Meditate on who you are in Christ and thank God for every good thing that is in you in Christ (Philemon 6). Remember the benefits and goodness of the Lord and give Him praise (Psalm 103:2).

There is joy and peace that comes from believing (Romans

15:13). Declare before God "I am a believer and I believe God's Word concerning me. The Lord is perfecting that which concerns me (Psalm 138:8). The Lord is on my side (Psalm 118:6). The Lord is for me, so who can be against me (Romans 8:31). The Lord is looking out for my good all the time (Romans 8:28), and I trust the Lord at all times. I am a believer and not a doubter."

The epistles also teach that our joy is made complete as we fellowship together (2 John 12; 1 John 1:3,4; 2 Timothy 1:4). So make it a habit to assemble together with other believers and incite and stimulate each other to love and to good deeds. Encourage and urge one another, especially in the last days, for these are indeed perilous times (Hebrews 10:24,25; 2 Timothy 3:1). As believers we have a responsibility to build each other up.

"Rejoice in the Lord always." Bind joy continually upon your heart. Refuse to be terrified by your enemy. "The joy of the Lord is your strength." If the devil cannot steal your joy then he would not be able to access your life.

Why Tithe?

As a minister, I must represent God to the people. I am not to speak my own opinion. Rather, I am to speak and write with the fear of God upon me, as a messenger of the Lord (Malachi 2:6; Galatians 1:10). I realize that this subject of tithing is a controversial subject, nevertheless it is important.

Let me begin by asking a series of questions. I trust that by the end of this article you will be able to answer each of these questions accurately, in accordance to God's Word. Each of us in our natural mind is affected by the reasoning of men, our fears and our emotions. Let us, however, lay all those things aside and approach this subject of tithing, desiring only the mind of God.

1. Does tithing have anything to do with the Lordship of Jesus in my life?
2. Is tithe holy?
3. Does the tithe belong to God?
4. Who owns the tithe, God or me?
5. Did tithing begin with the Law of Moses or did tithing exist before the Law?
6. Did tithing cease with the New Covenant?
7. Does tithing have anything to do with the worship of God?
8. When I tithe, am I honouring the Lord?
9. Does my tithing please God?
10. Does tithing have anything to do with my covenant with God?
11. Does my tithe have anything to do with my obedience?
12. Is tithing an act of faith in God as my source?
13. Does fear have any effect in the thinking and emotion of those who do not tithe?
14. Is the lack of the desire to tithe, a result of fear that one's needs will not be met? Or a fear that the church will misuse the tithe?

My prayer is that this article will not bring condemnation to you but rather truth and liberty.

Colossians 1:17, 18 says: Jesus existed before all things and in Him all things consist. He is the head of the church and He is your head so that in everything He should stand first and be pre-eminent. Tithing puts Jesus first. Adam got into trouble because he did not put God first. He did not honour or respect God by obeying the Lord's command! He took what belonged to the Lord and brought a curse upon himself, his family and all creation (Genesis 2:16, 17).

What is the Principle of Tithing?

The principle of tithing is seen as far back as the book of Genesis. Tithing is giving God the first and the best of your increase. When you tithe you open the door to the supernatural help, favour, and blessings of God (Proverbs 3:9,10). When you do not tithe you demonstrate to God that you do not think highly of His grace that enables you to obtain substance. In this, you open the door to the curse (Proverbs 26:2; Malachi 3:8, 9). It's not that God is *sending* the curse, but rather the curse is in the earth as a result of the fall.

Now Christ has legally redeemed you from the curse and brought you into the blessings. However you must work this out by faith and the fear of the Lord. You must not give any place to the devil. First Peter 5:8 says: the devil is the devourer, looking for who he may devour. But God says that when you tithe He will rebuke the devourer on your behalf (Malachi 3:11). So then, when you do not tithe you become one of those whom Satan may devour.

The curse came on Adam because he did not give God first place. God is the same; He has not changed (Malachi 3:6). God's principle is: if you demonstrate faithfulness over a little He will make you ruler over much. If Adam was faithful and obedient over God's tree, he would have been ruler over the whole earth and all the works of God's hands (Hebrews 2:7). There is an anointing to prosper that is activated in your life when you tithe correctly. It is a blessing—supernatural help that causes you to prosper and adds no sorrow with it (Proverbs 10:22).

If Adam had simply obeyed, an anointing, empowerment,

and blessing would have been released into his life, causing him to be:

1. Fruitful   - multiple harvests
2. Multiply   - increase numerically
3. Replenish   - to complete
4. Subdue   - to cause things to be subject to him
5. Dominate   - have dominion over, rule as king
               (Genesis 1:28)

This same anointing is available to you when you tithe (2 Corinthians 9:8). The principle of tithing existed before the law. Cain killed Abel over the issue of tithing and offering (Genesis 4:4-8). I believe Cain and Abel were taught tithing by their father, Adam. In Genesis 14:20, we see Abraham giving tithes to Melchizedek, priest of the Most High God. This came before the Law. Hebrews chapter seven teaches that Melchizedek was a type of Christ. Jesus is your Melchizedek—High Priest of the Most High God. Here on earth Melchizedek received tithes from Abraham on God's behalf. Today, the pastor (leader of the local church) receives tithe on Jesus' behalf (Hebrews 7:8).

Tithing is a question of obedience, giving God first place, honouring Jesus' Lordship, and worshiping God. Pharaoh of Egypt got into trouble with God because he refused to release God's firstborn—Israel (Exodus 4:22, 23). When Abraham was going to offer up Isaac, his firstborn, in obedience to God, he said *"I and the lad, will go yonder to worship"* (Genesis 22:5). Tithing is both obedience and worship. The Bible says to love God with all your might, even in the new and better covenant. What is your might? It is your substance, your finances, and your wealth. Tithing is loving God. Expressing your love to God, in obedience is part of the new covenant (John 14:21,23).

Tithing is also about Lordship. What is Lordship? Lordship is an attitude of reverence to God. It is honouring and obeying the Lord (Malachi 1:6). It is surrendering your will to Him. Lordship is intimacy with God. Lordship is looking to God as your source (Psalm 123:2). Lordship is conducting yourself in thought, word and deed, in a manner that is worthy of the Lord (Colossians 1:10; Psalm 50:23).

Tithing is the process by which you handle the tithe. The tithe is holy (Leviticus 27:30, 32). Communion is holy, yet tithing is nonetheless just as holy. You should come before the communion table with reverence and the fear of the Lord. Similarly, tithing involves the fear of the Lord (Malachi 1:6).

You tithe because you love God, honour God, and desire to obey and please Him. You also tithe in faith because God is a rewarder (Hebrews 11:6) and He says that He will open the windows of Heaven for those who tithe (Malachi 3:10). So you are supposed to tithe with the expectation that you will receive insight, better ways of doing things, supernatural help and blessings. You tithe in faith believing God to be your source. Abraham experienced that as recorded in Genesis 15:1. When you tithe you are trusting and obeying God; that is the fear of the Lord. Malachi 2:5 says the fear of the Lord is your responsibility in the covenant. God's part of the covenant is to provide peace, wholeness, and abundant life. Here is the fact: tithing activates your covenant! If your life experience is lack and oppression from the enemy you cannot afford not to tithe (Haggai 1:2-11).

Now is a good time to go back and answer those previous

questions from a biblical stand-point.

The truth will bring liberty (John 8:32). Jesus practiced and taught tithing, He said: *"when you tithe, not if you tithe, do so in love, mercy, faith and justice"* (Luke 11:42; Matthew 23:23). Tithing is right. Tithing is part of God's system to make sure the financial needs in His house are met (Malachi 3:10; Nehemiah 13:10-12). The church is called a holy nation (1 Peter 2:9). God said in Malachi 3:9: "You have robbed me, even the whole nation".

Studies show that the majority of the church do not tithe. Studies also show that hundreds of billions of dollars pass through the lives of believers' of North America each year. Where did those billions go? They are sitting in secular banks, dominated by the devil's system, making sinners rich, and financing Satan's operations. However, we are in the last days, and a wealth transfer will take place (Proverbs 13:22; James 5:1-7). Those billions will remain in the church and pay for the work of the Lord; souls will be reached for the kingdom of God! There will be a collapse of this world's financial system. You need to be involved in God's financial programs. Tithing gets you hooked up in God's prosperity system (Matthew 6:20; 1 Timothy 6:18, 19).

If you are a tither, I encourage you to get more involved in the tithing process with your heart, faith, fear of the Lord, and love. If you are a backslidden tither, now is a good time to get back on track. If you are not a tither, get over the fear and choose to tithe; it is a choice *you* can make. "The Lord will make you a delightsome land" (Malachi 3:12).

21 Reasons to Tithe:

1. Tithing hooks you up with God's system of

prosperity (Genesis 1:28).

2. Tithing aligns you with God's priorities (Psalms 35:27; Psalms 122: 6-9; Deuteronomy 8:18).

3. Tithing connects you with God's covenant (Exodus 34:10-26). God will be El-Shaddai to you (Genesis 14:21-15:1; Joshua 7:1-12).

4. Tithing in the New Testament pleases God (Hebrews 7:7,8; John 15:12).

5. Jesus is your example (Matthew 23:23; Luke 11:42).

6. Tithing is loving God with all your might (1 Chronicles 29:2; Matthew 6:21; Deuteronomy 6:5).

7. Tithing is demonstrating Jesus' Lordship. Jesus says in Luke 6:46: "Why call me Lord and do not the things I say?"

8. Tithing acknowledges the preeminence of God and the fact that God owns everything (Psalm 50:12-15).

9. Tithing hooks you up with God's prosperity (Isaiah 1:19; Job 36:11).

10. Tithing opens the door for favour (Proverbs 3:4-10).

11. Tithing is worship and it involves giving your best to God because He is worthy (Exodus 4:22-23; Genesis 22:5, 12).

12. Tithing has a Godly purpose (Exodus 35:1-8;

Ephesians 2:19, 20; Malachi 3:10). Tithing helps build God's House—a house of people.

13. Tithing opens the door for revelation. The windows of Heaven will be opened so you may see what others cannot (Malachi 3:10).

14. Tithing opens the door to wealth (Psalms 112:1,3; Proverbs 8:21).

15. Tithing activates God's rebuke over the devil (Malachi 3:11; Proverbs 11:24, 25).

16. Tithing releases faith (1 Kings 17:8-16).

17. Tithing connects you with deliverance. Second Corinthians 9:8 says: all grace will abound toward you.

18. Tithing shuts the door to the curse (Malachi 3:8,9; Proverbs 26:2).

19. Tithing teaches you to trust God (Genesis 22:8).

20. Tithing releases God to be involved in your affairs (Ephesians 4:28-30).

21. Tithing is also an opportunity for you to thank God for what He has brought you through and where He is taking you (Deuteronomy 26).

Section II

Confessions

"Let God be true but every man a liar. As it is written: That You may be justified in Your words, And may overcome when You are judged" (Romans 3:4).

Section II: *Confessions*

A. Redemptive Truths

"And you shall know the truth, and the truth shall make you free" (John 8:32).

Redemption

Allow me to share with you a truthful word: the devil is a thief and a liar. The devil would like for you to live as if the truth of redemption was not so. He does not want you to benefit from the fullness of salvation which includes: healing, protection, prosperity, deliverance, fruits of the Spirit, righteousness, confidence, fellowship with God, authority, and total freedom. These all belong to you (Romans 5:17). However, you take hold of these things by faith. You must believe and confess them into manifestation. Where there is lack of understanding and ignorance, we are alienated from the *Zoë* life of God (Ephesians 4:18) and are paralyzed and perish for lack of knowledge (Hosea 4:6).

So, dear blood bought child of God, I encourage you to humbly (James 4:6) and aggressively (Matthews 11:12) lay hold of your redemption privileges as you meditate in this section "Redemptive Truths".

Portrait of the New Man

I am a new creation. I am God's workmanship created in Christ. I am an heir of God, Jesus is heir to all that the Father has, and I am a joint heir with Christ. All things are mine. When God gave me Jesus, He also freely gave me all things.

I am a king and a priest to God. I am born from above. Old things have passed away, all things have become new, and all things are of God. Everything that is in me is born of God and whatever is born of God overcomes the world. Everything in me is victorious over the world and all that the devil has.

I am created in righteousness and true holiness. I am blameless in Christ. I am sanctified and set apart for God. I belong to God. I am the temple of God. God lives on the inside of me. And "greater is He that is in me than he that is in the world."

Christ is my wisdom, redemption, sanctification, and righteousness. In fact, Christ is my life. I am crucified with Christ, and it is no longer I that live, but Christ lives His life in me and through me. I have the mind of Christ. The kingdom of God is in me. The love of God is shed abroad in my heart. I have a measure of God's faith in me. I am a believer and not a doubter. I am blessed with all spiritual blessing in Christ. I have an inheritance in Christ. I have been made rich in Christ. The glory of God is in me. Now, I am a son of God. I am accepted. I am redeemed from the curse, poverty, sickness, and death.

I have the right to the name of Jesus and all authority that is in Jesus' name. In the name of Jesus, I am a master over devils, demons, and circumstances. I am raised up with Christ and I sit in heavenly places at the right hand of my Father, in Christ. The throne of God backs me up. I am anointed. I am called and chosen. The light and the life of God are in me now. I am in God and God is in me. I can do all things through Christ who enables me. God is on my side and is always working for my good. My Father loves me as much as He loves Jesus, and I am more than a conqueror through Him.

(2 Corinthians 5:17; Ephesians 2:10; Romans 8:17; Hebrews 1:3; 1 Corinthians 3:21; Romans 8:32; Revelation 1:6; 2 Corinthians 5:17-18; 1 John 5:4; Ephesians 4:24; Colossians 1:22; 1 Corinthians 6:19-20; 1 John 4:4; 1 Corinthians 1:30; Colossians 3:4; Galatians 2:20; 1 Corinthians 2:16; Luke 17:21; Romans 5:5; Romans 12:3;

Ephesians 1:3; Ephesians 1:11; 2 Corinthians 4:7; Colossians 1:27; 1 John 3:2; Ephesians 1:6; Galatians 3:13; John 14:12; Mark 16:17; Ephesians 2:6; 2 Corinthians 1:21; John 8:12; Acts 17:28; Philippians 4:13; Romans 8:31; Romans 8:28; John 17:23; Romans 8:37)

The Reality of Redemption

When the truth of God's Word becomes a reality in my heart, it will make me free. It will prevail over circumstances and produce freedom and liberty in my life.

In regards to my redemption, I do know the grace of my Lord Jesus Christ, that though He was rich, for my sake He became poor, that I through His poverty might be made rich.

Christ was made a curse for me, "for it is written; cursed is every one that hangs on a tree." Christ has redeemed me from the curse of the Law. Christ became everything I was, so that I might become everything He is. Jesus took my place on the cross. He became sin so that now I am the righteousness of God in Christ. He took all my sickness and disease so that now divine healing is mine. He became poor so that now I am rich. He was despised, rejected, and forsaken, so that now I am accepted. Therefore, God will never leave me nor forsake me.

Christ took my shame and guilt so that now I have glory and a blood-washed conscience before my Father God. Jesus took my condemnation so that now I am justified and have peace with God. Jesus was cut out of the presence of God so I can be accepted into the presence of my Holy Father. I have His presence on the inside of me. Jesus bore my weakness that I may be strong in the Lord and in the power of His might. Jesus tasted death so I might have the *Zoë* life of God. Jesus went to Hell so that Heaven is now my home. Surely I am delivered from the power of darkness and I am now in the kingdom of Christ—the kingdom of Light. In Christ I have obtained an eternally perfected redemption through the precious blood of Jesus. I am rescued and delivered from sin and all its penalty. Praise God I am redeemed and I can say so. As He is, so am I in this world.

(John 8:32; Acts 19:20; 2 Corinthians 8:9; Galatians 3:13; Hebrews 2:14-15; 2 Corinthians 5:21; Isaiah 53:3-5; Matthew 8:17; Hebrews 13:5; Matthew 28:20; Hebrews 12:2; Colossians 1:27; Hebrews 2:10; Hebrews 9:14; Romans 8:1; Romans 5:1; Matthew 27:46; Ephesians 1:6; Hebrews 10:19; 2 Corinthians 6:16; Ephesians 6:10; Hebrews 2:9; John 5:24; Acts 2:27; John 14:2-3; Colossians 1:13; Hebrews 9:12; Psalm 107:2; 1 John 4:17)

Redemption is Mine

Jesus is the Lamb God provided as my perfect sacrifice on the cross (John 1:29). I am totally redeemed from the authority and dominion of Satan (Colossians 1:13). I have been made the very righteousness of God in Christ (2 Corinthians 5:21).

Jesus fulfilled every righteous requirement of the law (Matthew 5:17; Romans 8:4). Jesus is the Lamb of God without spot or blemish (1 Peter 1:19). He is my perfect substitute. Jesus took my sins and sicknesses upon Himself (Isaiah 53:4,5). He took my fallen sin nature in His Spirit and became sin for me (2 Corinthians 5:21; John 3:14). He bore my shame, guilt, and poverty (2 Corinthians 8:9). His soul and Spirit went into the very pits of hell on my behalf (Matthew 12:39-40). Jesus suffered unimaginable torment in my place (Isaiah 53:10), and met the demands of justice (Isaiah 53:11). When the price was fully paid for my redemption, Jesus was made alive spiritually in the very bowels of hell (Acts 13:33; Hebrews 1:5, 6; Colossians 1:18; 1 Peter 3:18; Revelation 1:5). Jesus, the last Adam, as a born again new creation man, stripped Satan of his authority over the human race (Colossians 2:15). He paralyzed the devil's death dealing power (Hebrews 2:14), and took from him the keys of hell and death (Revelation 1:18), on my behalf and in my place. Jesus' victory over the enemy is my victory. I identify completely with Christ's substitution work on my behalf.

Jesus was raised up from the dead by the glory of the Father (Ephesians 1:19-20; Romans 6:4). Jesus picked up His glorified and immortal body. He ascended into Heaven and took His blood into the Holiest of Holies where it was received and accepted by God the Father, thus sealing my eternal redemption (Hebrews 9:12), and establishing the New Covenant. Jesus took His place at the right hand of the Father, the throne of God Almighty, and there He sits as my High Priest, my Advocate, and He ever lives to make intercession for me (Hebrews 8:1; 7:25). I am not just a servant of God; I am now a son of God (John 1:12; Romans 8:14-17).

I identify completely with Christ as my substitute. In the mind of God, I am crucified with Christ (Galatians 2:20), I died with Christ (Romans 6:8), I was buried with Christ (Colossians 2:12), I am justified with Christ (1 Timothy 3:16), I am made alive with Christ (Colossians 2:13), I am raised up with Christ, I am made to sit with Christ in His throne at the right hand of the Father (Ephesians 2:6), I am completely, totally, and eternally redeemed from the hands of the enemy (Colossians 1:13; Ephesians 1:7; Hebrews 9:12), I am a son of God (1 John 3:2), and I am an overcomer (Revelation 3:21).

Jesus' redemption is for the whole world. I will tell others this Good News, so they can choose Jesus as their Lord and receive their redemption and become the righteousness of God in Christ (2 Corinthians 5:19-20).

Put on the New Man

When I believed on Jesus and confessed Him as my Lord, I was born again, I received eternal life, and I passed from spiritual death to life (John 5:24). I am now a new man on the inside (2 Corinthians 5:17-18). I am a son of God through faith in Christ Jesus. When I was baptized into Christ, I was clothed with Christ on the inside (Galatians 3:26-27). God is presently at work in me, filling me with His thoughts, His desires, and His will (Philippians 2:13). I am confident that the good work God began in me, He will also complete and bring to perfection (Philippians 1:6).

I work out my salvation with fear and trembling (Philippians 2:12), and I put on the new man on the outside. I lay aside the old man, which is corrupted in accordance with the lusts of deceit (Ephesians 4:22). I strip off the old self with his carnal thinking, his selfish attitudes, and his fleshly desires. I put on the new man, which in the likeness of God, has been created in righteousness and true holiness (Ephesians 4:24).

I let this attitude be in me, which was also in Christ Jesus (Philippians 2:5). I refuse to be conformed to the world's way of thinking (Romans 12:2). I will not live a purposeless life as the Gentiles do (Ephesians 4:17). The whole spirit and attitude of my mind is being renewed to be in conformity to the new man that I am (Ephesians 4:23). I set my affections and thoughts on the things which are above, not on the things that are on earth (Colossians 3:1).

I acknowledge every good thing that is in me in Christ (Philemon 6). I rehearse the benefits of my salvation (Psalm 103:2). My life is full of what I consistently say with my mouth (Proverbs 18:20). I put on the new man by thinking, speaking, and acting in ways that are in harmony with who I really am in Christ (Colossians 3:10). I put on the Lord Jesus Christ, and I put a stop to gratifying the evil desires of my earthly nature (Romans 13:14). I discipline my body to obey my inner man, the real me (1 Corinthians 9:27). I commit to being continually filled with the Word (Colossians 3:16), and the Spirit (Ephesians 5:18). I purpose to live in the Spirit (Galatians 5:25), walk in the Spirit (Galatians 5:16), and be led by the Spirit (Romans 8:14).

My new garments fit rightly when I put off the old man and put on the new man. I put on the garments of praise and salvation (Isaiah 61:3,10). I clothe myself with humility (1 Peter 5:5). I clothe myself with zeal as a cloak (Isaiah 59:17), and I cover myself with the robe of righteousness (Isaiah 61:10). I will remember to put on the new man.

Total Identification Confession

I am crucified with Christ. I identify with Him in His suffering and shame on the cross. Jesus was made sin with my sin. By the faith of the operation of God (Colossians 2:12), God placed me upon Christ so that I died with Him and was buried with Him (Romans 6:4). Jesus took my place on the cross. My sin was the reason for the crown of thorns that pierced His brow, stripped Him naked, drove the nails into

His hands and feet, and pierced His side with a Roman sword. He died in my place, taking the punishment that I should have taken.

Because of His love, He submitted to the authority of darkness, sin, and spiritual death, and as Moses lifted up the serpent in the wilderness, even so Jesus was lifted up on the cross (John 3:14). Identifying with the enemy, Satan, He became as a worm (Psalm 22:6).

Oh, how I identify with Christ. It was my sin, my sickness, my poverty, my curse, my spiritual death that He partook of. He suffered there in the bowels of Hell, and in the midst of all that torment, the jeers from the demons, and the wrath of God poured out, He suffered there until the claims of justice against me had been fully satisfied and there were no longer any charges against me.

My spiritual death and union with Satan was broken and wiped out. Jesus was justified in the spirit (1 Timothy 3:16). His justification was for me. Jesus went to Hell on my behalf. He went because of my sin, not His own. Jesus was my perfect substitute. When Jesus was made alive in the Spirit I was made alive (1 Peter 3:18). Jesus spoiled principalities and powers (Colossians 2:15). It was *my* victory over the Devil and his demons.

When Jesus was raised up, I was raised up together with Him. When Jesus was made to sit at the right hand of the Father, I was made to sit together with Him. Jesus' victory is my victory. I share His authority. His authority is my authority. That's why I have His name. This is the truth. I am victorious over Hell, death, the grave, Satan, sin, demons, sickness, poverty, and every curse. Praise the Lord!

I am a new creation (2 Corinthians 5:17). I am the

workmanship of God in Christ (Ephesians 2:10). I've been created in righteousness and true holiness (Ephesians 4:24).

(The above confession is adapted from E.W. Kenyon's writing.)

My True Identity
(Based on Romans Chapter 6)

I have been baptized into Christ; therefore, I have put on Christ (Galatians 3:27). Christ is my life and identification. I have been baptized into His death. My old man and all his selfish and sinful deeds are buried with Christ by baptism into His death. Like Christ I was also raised up (spiritually) from the dead by the glory of the Father. I now should walk in the newness of my new life in Christ. This I know, the old man is crucified with Christ, so that the body of sin might be destroyed and rendered powerless. I should no longer serve sin or live a life apart from God and His glory.

I declare the old man is dead. He that is dead is free from sin. I am raised with Christ and I share His life, His anointing, and His authority. Christ being raised from the dead dies no more. Death has no power over Him. I identify totally with Christ. I identify with His death, burial, resurrection, ascension, and His seating at the place of ultimate authority at the right hand of God the Father. Death has no power over me.

I am dead to sin and live in an unbroken fellowship with my Father God. I refuse to allow sin to reign in my mortal body by obeying its lust and passions. I yield my thoughts, my will, my members, and my whole being to God as instruments of righteousness, working in harmony with God, for His purposes. Sin shall not dominate me. Christ in me has fulfilled every requirement of the law for me. The law therefore has no legal demand on me. I am not under the law but under grace. I am not under condemnation but I am yoked to justification.

Where sin abounded, grace abounds much more through the life of Christ and the anointing of God in me. I obey God, not sin. My members are servants of righteousness leading to holiness. No addiction or bad habit can dominate me anymore. I know the Truth. Christ the anointed in me is the Truth. The truth sets me free. I am free indeed (John 8:32, 36). Hallelujah!

The communication of my faith becomes effective by the acknowledging of every good thing, which is in me in Christ (Philemon 6).

Christ is My Life

"When Christ, who is my life, shall appear, then shall I also appear with Him in Glory" (Colossians 3:4). *"The Lord is my rock, and my fortress, and my deliverer; my God, my strength, in whom I trust; my buckler, and the horn of my salvation, and my high tower"* (Psalm 18:2). *"The Lord is my light"* (Psalm 27:1), my peace, my exceeding joy, my righteousness, my wisdom, my redemption, my sanctification (1 Corinthians 1:30), and my health. I have been baptized into Christ and I have put on Christ (Galatians 3:27). I make no provision for the flesh to fulfill the lusts thereof (Romans 13:14). Christ is my self-control and temperance. Old things have passed away, all things become new and all things are of God (2 Corinthians 5:17). Christ is my security and success. I walk and live according to the law of the Spirit of Life in Christ Jesus (Romans 8: 2). I am complete in Him, Who is the head

of all principality and power (Colossians 2:10). I have the faith of Christ. I have what I say! I am to God a sweet savor of Christ (2 Corinthians 2:15). *"Now thanks be unto God Who always causes me to triumph in Christ"* (2 Corinthians 2:14).

Reality of Righteousness

All my sins, sicknesses, and iniquities were laid on Jesus (Isaiah 53: 4,5). Jesus was made to be sin for me. When I confessed Jesus as my Lord and Saviour, I was made the very righteousness of God in Christ (2 Corinthians 5:21). All my sins and iniquities have been completely wiped out (Hebrews 10:17,18). The righteousness of God that I now have has given me a right stance before a Holy and a Righteous God. I am free from guilt, condemnation and any consciousness of sin (Romans 8:1; Hebrews 10:2). I can come boldly into the presence of my awesome Holy Creator (Hebrews 10:19). God finds no fault in me. I have been made Holy and blameless through the Blood of Christ (Colossians 1:22). My righteousness is perfect. I am found in Christ not having my own righteousness, based on the law or my own works. But, through faith in Christ and His finished work of redemption, I am found in Christ having the perfect righteousness of God (Philippians 3:9).

When I received Jesus as my Lord and Saviour, God gave me the right to become His very own son (John 1:12). God sent forth the Spirit of His Son into my heart, crying, Daddy, Father (Galatians 4:6). I have received the Spirit of Adoption (Romans 8: 15). The Righteousness of God brought me into son-ship with God Almighty. I can now have perfect fellowship with God as my Father, without any sense of inferiority (1 John 1:3).

Jesus defeated the devil on my behalf. Jesus stripped the devil of his authority and broke his dominion over me (Hebrews 2:14; Colossians 2:15). Jesus' victory is mine. I am not only delivered from the devils dominion (Colossians 1:13), but in the name of Jesus I am also a master of the devil and all his works (Luke 10:19; Matthew 28:18; Revelation 1: 18). My righteousness, which is of God, gave me a right stance before the enemy. I stand as an overcomer (1 John 5:5), a victor (1 Corinthians 15: 57), and more than a conqueror (Romans 8:37) over the devil. The devil is eternally defeated and I am eternally redeemed (Hebrews 9:12).

My righteousness also gave me rights. I am a citizen of Heaven (Ephesians 2:18,19) with rights and privileges. I am a joint heir with Christ (Romans 8:17). All things are mine (1 Corinthians 3:21; Hebrews 1: 3; Ephesians 1: 3; Romans 8: 32; 2 Peter 1:3).

I receive my righteousness and reign as a king in this life through Christ Jesus (Romans 5:17). Christ is filling me with His righteousness day by day. I am being established in righteousness (Isaiah 54:14). "No weapon formed against me shall prosper." I am a son of God and my righteousness is of God my Father (Isaiah 54:17).

Righteous Consciousness

Jesus, having purged me from my sins, has enabled me to stand in the presence of the Heavenly Father, Who is holy, without any consciousness of sin. By the offering of the body of Jesus Christ, and His shed blood, I am sanctified and perfected forever. I have no consciousness of sins, shame, or guilt; old things are passed away, all things are become new. I am a new creation in Christ. I am born again and made the righteousness of God in Christ. I have communion, union, and fellowship with my Father God, and my Lord Jesus Christ through the power of the Holy Spirit. I am one with the Father, the Son, the Holy Spirit and the church. Furthermore, I am seated in Christ on His throne, at the right hand of my heavenly Father.

(Hebrews 1:3; Hebrews 10: 2,10,14; Hebrews 9:14; 2 Corinthians 5:17; 1 John 1:3; John 17:20; Hebrews 10:12; Ephesians 2: 6)

Realities of the New Creation

It has been said, 'I am just a sinner saved by grace.' I was a sinner, I was saved by God's grace, and now I am sanctified in Christ, and called a saint (1 Corinthians 1:2). For too long, I have been held captive to a sense of unworthiness and inferiority. As a result, I was robbed of my confidence, my faith, and my fellowship with my Father God. I am the righteousness of God in Christ (2 Corinthians 5:21). I will no longer allow a sin conscious mindset to pollute and dominate me.

God my Father says, I am His workmanship, created in Christ Jesus (Ephesians 2:10). My Father calls me by numerous uplifting names, and I answer to them. He calls me: His son (1 John 3:2), My righteous one (Hebrews 10:38), holy priesthood (1 Peter 2:5), king (Revelation 1:6), ambassador of Christ (2 Corinthians 5:20), His temple (2 Corinthians 6:16), joint-heir (Romans 8:17), citizen of Heaven (Ephesians 2:19), branch of the Vine (John 15:5), and more. My Father sees me as precious in His sight (Isaiah 43:4). So precious, that He purchased me for Himself with the Blood of His only begotten Son Jesus (1 Corinthians 6:20). I will never again receive the devil's lies that I am unworthy. I was born of the will of God (John 1:13), the Spirit of God (John 3:6), and the Word of God (1 Peter 1:23).

I do understand that where there is no vision the people perish (Proverbs 29:18), because as a man thinks in his heart so he becomes (Proverbs 23:7). I receive and I am becoming more pregnant day by day with the image of the new creation that I am. I have a new identity. Jesus is my new life and identity (Colossians 3:4; Galatians 2:20; 2 Corinthians 3:18).

The brand new person that I am is created in righteousness and true holiness (Ephesians 4:24). I have received God's own nature (2 Peter 1:4). I have eternal life (1 John 5:13; John 5:24). God's creative ability is in me (John 1:4; 8:12). God's creative faith is in me (Romans 12:3; Hebrews 11:3). God is in me (1 John 4:4). I am hooked up with omnipotence (Ephesians 1:18-19). I can do all things through Christ that enables me (Philippians 4:13). I know no limitations. Christ is my wisdom, righteousness, sanctification, and redemption (1 Corinthians 1:30). The all-powerful Name of Jesus belongs to me (Matthew 16:19; John 14:13). In the Name of Jesus, I have authority over devils, demons, sickness, sin, and poverty (Luke 10:19; Mark 16:17). I am a supernatural man in Christ. Nothing is impossible to me (Matthew 17:20). Now I will stand fast in this liberty wherewith Christ has made me completely free and will not be held again with a yoke of bondage (Galatians 5:1).

Free in Jesus' Name

In Jesus' name, I am free indeed. Jesus has set me free. Sickness cannot dwell in me. When I use Jesus' name, I present all that Jesus is. I, therefore, resist sickness, pain, poverty, and lack in the name of Jesus. In the name of Jesus,

God is causing me to triumph over every problem. Every mountain shall be removed. As a child of God, I have the right to use the name of Jesus. I will use the name of Jesus against the enemies of my soul. In the name of Jesus, I have all sufficiency. I have access to Heaven's provision for me. In the name of Jesus, I possess my inheritance in Christ. In Jesus' name I resist fear. Praise the Lord!

Section II: *Confessions*

B. The Blood of Christ

"Now may the God of peace who brought up our Lord Jesus from the dead, that great Shepherd of the sheep, through the blood of the everlasting covenant, make you complete in every good work to do His will, working in you what is well pleasing in His sight, through Jesus Christ, to whom be glory forever and ever. Amen" (Hebrews 13:20-21).

The Blood of Christ

Whenever I stand accused by the enemy of my soul, the shed Blood of Christ rises to my defense to speak on my behalf (Hebrews 12:24). The Blood declares that I am innocent, forgiven, and justified (Ephesians 1:7; Romans 3:24). All charges against me must be dropped and I must go free, because whom the Son has set free is free indeed (John 8:36).

When circumstances seem overwhelming and are predicting my defeat, the Blood of Christ speaks to me and says, "All the promises of God belong to you" (Exodus 24:8; Hebrews 9:19). The Father's answer to every one of those promises in Christ is a divine, yes, and Amen (2 Corinthians 1:20). With this assurance, I rise up in faith. With the promises of God in my mouth, I speak to the mountains and circumstances in the name of Jesus, and I overcome them by the Blood of the Lamb and the Word of my testimony (Revelation 12:11).

When sickness or poverty comes to my door, the Blood of Christ on my doorposts answers and rebukes the curse saying, 'Pass over this child of God; pass over this family. They are the redeemed of the Lord' (Galatians 3:13; Exodus 12:13). When my children go to school, I plead the Blood of Christ on them. When fear attacks, I plead the Blood of Christ. In every circumstance, the Blood of Christ is my defense.

The voice of the Blood of Christ is heard in Heaven, earth, and under the earth (Philippians 2:10). The devil is eternally defeated because of the Blood of Christ (Hebrews 9:12). I am more than a conqueror through Christ Jesus because of His Blood (Romans 8:37).

Because of the Blood of Christ

If we receive the witness of men, the witness of God is greater (I John 5:9). We have come to Mount Zion, and to the city of the living God, the heavenly Jerusalem, and to an innumerable company of angels, to the general assembly and church of the first born who are registered in Heaven, and to God the Judge of all, to the spirits of just men made perfect, to Jesus the Mediator of the new covenant, and to the blood of sprinkling, that speaks better things than that of Abel (Hebrews 12:22-24).

Because of faith in the Blood (Romans 3:25), I am made the righteousness of God in Christ (2 Corinthians 5:21). Because of faith in the Blood I can come boldly to the throne of grace that I may obtain mercy and find grace to help in time of need (Hebrews 4:16). The life of the flesh is in the blood (Leviticus 17:11). When my Father God sees the Blood of Christ on the altar of the mercy seat, He sees the life of His Son, Jesus, Who was obedient even to death (Philippians 2:8), given as a sacrifice for me.

Because of the Blood, I am reconciled to God. I have redemption, wholeness, righteousness, forgiveness, restoration, and prosperity. Foreshadowing the sacrifice of Christ, Moses took the blood and sprinkled the people and the books and said: *"Behold the blood of the covenant, which the Lord has made with you concerning all these words"* (Exodus 24:8). I therefore declare that *all the promises of God in Him are yes and in Him Amen, to the glory of God through us* (2 Corinthians 1:20). *"Grace and peace are multiplied to me through the knowledge of God, and of Jesus my Lord, according as His divine power has given to me all things that pertain to life and godliness, through the knowledge of Him that has called me to glory and virtue, whereby are given to me exceeding great and precious promises that by these I might be a partaker of His divine nature having escaped the corruption that is in the world through lust"* (2 Peter 1:2-4).

There is deliverance and protection because of the Blood, for it is written, *"When I see the blood I will pass over You"* (Exodus 12:13). The Blood of Jesus is the seal of my deliverance from the enemies' dominion and the signature on the document of the new covenant guaranteeing my victory over all the works of the enemy (Luke 10:19). *"For Jesus having spoiled principalities and powers He made a show of them openly, triumphing over them in it"* (Colossians 2:15). *"I have been delivered from the power of darkness, and translated into the kingdom of Christ in whom I have redemption through His blood even the forgiveness of sins"* (Colossians 1:13,14).

I have overcome the devil, by the Blood of the Lamb and the Word of my testimony, and I loved not my life even to death (Revelation 12:11). The Blood of Jesus symbolizes the obedience of Christ even to death. *"Wherefore God also hath highly exalted Him, and given Him a name which is above every name: That at the name of Jesus every knee should bow, of things in heaven, and things in the earth, and things under the earth"* (Philippians 2:9-10). All power in Heaven and earth has been given to Jesus and is in His name (Matthew 28:18). Jesus said, *"I am He that lives and was dead and behold I am alive forevermore. Amen; and I have the keys of hell and of death"* (Revelation 1:18). There is power in the name of Jesus because of the absolute obedience of Jesus as expressed by His Blood. Because of the Blood of Jesus, in the name of Jesus, I have power to tread upon serpents and nothing can by any means hurt me (Luke 10:19). I have been given the keys of the kingdom of Heaven and whatever I shall bind in earth shall be bound in Heaven and whatever I shall loosen on earth shall be loosened in Heaven (Matthew 18:18).

I have a new and a better covenant, established upon better promises, having a better priesthood and better sacrifices (Hebrews 8:6; 9:23).This new covenant is in force because the testator has died (Hebrews 9:17). The proof is in the blood. The testator is also risen from the dead and sits at the right hand of the Father as the Apostle and High priest of my profession, enforcing my covenant rights (Hebrews 3:1).

Discerning the Blood of Christ

Jesus is my propitiation through faith in His Blood (Romans 3:25). In Him my sins are not only forgiven but they are remitted (Hebrews 9:22). *"As far as the east is from the west so far has he removed my transgressions"* (Psalm 103:12) The handwriting of ordinances that was against me has been taken out of the way, having been nailed to His cross (Colossians 2:14). I am now justified by His Blood and shall be saved from wrath to come (Romans 5:9; 1 Thessalonians 1:10). Not by the blood of goats and calves, but by His own Blood, Jesus entered in once into the Holy place, having obtained eternal redemption for me (Hebrews 9:12).

Christ through His death destroyed the devil who had the power of death and has delivered them who through the fear of death were all their lifetime subject to bondage (Hebrews 2:14-15). For this purpose, the Son of God was manifested, that He might destroy the works of the devil (1 John 3:8).

I can walk in the light as He is in the light because the Blood of Jesus cleanses me from all sin (1 John 1:7). I can walk in truth. I am redeemed not with corruptible things as silver and gold from my vain conversations received by traditions from my fathers, but by the precious Blood of Christ as a Lamb without blemish and without spot. I am free from vanity (1 Peter 1:18-19).

What's more, the Blood of Jesus has made atonement for my soul (Leviticus 11:11). The Blood of Christ, Who through the eternal Spirit offered Himself without spot to God, purges my conscience from dead works, guilt, and condemnations to serve God (Hebrews 9:14), in righteousness and truth, having a pure conscience undefiled before God (Acts 24:16).

The Blood is the assurance of the Father's love for me. For while I was yet a sinner, Christ died for me (Romans 5:8). I am persuaded of Jesus' love, His faithfulness, and His commitment to me. He has made me a King and a priest unto God Who is His Father and my Father, having loved me and washed me from my sins in His own Blood. *"To Him be glory and dominion forever and ever. Amen!"* (Revelation 1:6)

I am bought with a price (1 Corinthians 6:20). I belong to God. I am sanctified and separated unto God for His purpose. I will glorify Him in my body and in my spirit which are God's (1 Corinthians 6:20). I honour the Blood by walking in fellowship and communion with the Blood (1 Corinthians 10:16). The consecration of my God is upon my head. All the days of my separation I am holy unto the Lord (Numbers 6:7,8). I therefore honour the Blood by walking in the fear of the Lord, in obedience, in love, and in faith. May the God of peace, that brought again from the dead my Lord Jesus, that great Shepherd of the sheep, through the Blood of the everlasting covenant, make me perfect in every good work to do His will working in me that which is well pleasing in His sight through Jesus Christ to whom be glory forever and ever. Amen (Hebrews 13:20-21).

I am made one with believers in Christ Jesus through the Blood. We, who were sometimes far off, are made near by the Blood of Christ (Ephesians 2:13). The wall of partition has been broken down. The walls of racial differences, gender barriers, economic divisions, and language barriers have all been broken down. Jesus is our peace Who has made us one. We are reconciled in Him in one body by the Cross, having slain the enmity in Himself (Ephesians 2:6). In Christ we are built together for a holy habitation of God through the Spirit (Ephesians 2:22).

Jesus is the propitiation not for my own sins only, but for the sins of the whole world (I John 2:2). Jesus gave Himself a ransom for all (1 Timothy 2:6). I have the right to believe for the salvation of my family, friends, city, and for the curse to be broken off the entire earth and all of God's creation (Romans 8:21; Revelation 22:3). The price has been paid for every captive to go free. He said, because of the Blood of the covenant I will set your prisoners free (Zechariah 9:11).

The Blood of Christ guarantees the full redemption of my body at His appearing. It does not yet appear what I shall be, but I know that when He shall appear I shall be like Him (I John 3:2). I shall have a body like His glorious body (Philippians 3:21). Jesus' second coming is guaranteed by His Blood, for unto them that look for Him shall He appear the second time without sin unto salvation (Hebrews 9:28).

Victory is mine because of faith in the Blood and reverence for the Blood of Christ. But woe unto those who transgress, disregard, and dishonour the Blood. He that despised Moses' law died without mercy under two or three witnesses. How much sorer punishment shall he be thought worthy who trodden under foot the Son of God, and counted the blood of the covenant, wherewith he was sanctified, an unholy thing, and has done despite unto the Spirit of grace. For we know Him that said vengeance is mine. The Lord shall judge His people. *"It is a fearful thing to fall into the hands of the living God"* (Hebrews 10:28-31).

My God is a consuming fire (Hebrews 12:29). He returns to battle on a white horse clothed with a vesture dipped in blood (Revelation 19:13). He is King of kings and Lord of lords, and out of His mouth goes a sword (Revelation 19:16,15). I will worship and bow down before Him. He is my Saviour and my Lord. He is my King. I will honour the Blood of the Lamb of God, that was slain before the foundation of the world (Revelation 13:8). Praise and glory to His Name. Amen!

Thanksgiving because of the Blood

Thank You, Father, for the Blood of Christ that is shed for me. Because of my faith in the Blood of Christ (Romans 3:25) I am made the righteousness of God in Christ (2 Corinthians 5:21). Thank You, Father, that when You see the Blood of Christ on the altar of the mercy seat You see the life of Your Son, Jesus, Who was obedient even unto death (Philippians 2:8), given as a sacrifice for me. Thank You, Father, that I can come boldly to the throne of grace, that I may obtain mercy and find grace to help me in time of need (Hebrews 4:16). Because of the Blood, I am reconciled to You. I have redemption, righteousness, and salvation (1 Corinthians 1:30). Jesus, You are my propitiation through faith in Your Blood (Romans 3:25).

Thank You, Father, that my sins are not only forgiven but they are remitted (Hebrews 9:22). As far as the east is from the west, so far You have removed my transgressions from me (Psalm 103:12). The handwriting of requirements that was against me has been taken out of the way, having been nailed to Jesus' cross (Colossians 2:14). My slate has been wiped clean. The old arrest warrant has been cancelled. I am now justified by the Blood of Christ and saved from the wrath to come (Romans 5:9; 1 Thessalonians 1:10). Not by the blood of goats and calves, but by His own Blood, Jesus entered in once into the Holy place having obtained eternal redemption for me (Hebrews 9:12). Thank You, Father, for my eternal redemption because of the Blood.

Thank You, Father, that I have a new and better covenant than the old covenant. Your new covenant is established upon better promises, having a better priesthood and better sacrifices (Hebrews 8:6). This new covenant is in order because Jesus the testator has died (Hebrews 9:17). The proof of His death is in the Blood. Jesus is also risen from the dead and sits at the right hand of the Majesty on high (Hebrews 1:3), as the Apostle and High Priest of my confession, overseeing my covenant rights (Hebrews 3:1). All Your promises have been sprinkled by the Blood of Christ and they belong to me. I have received exceeding great and precious promises that by these I do partake of Your divine nature and escape the corruption that is in the world through lust (2 Peter 1:2-4).

Thank You, Father, for deliverance and protection because of the Blood (Exodus 12:13). The Blood of Christ is the seal on my deliverance from the enemy's dominion. The Blood of Christ ratifies the document of the New Covenant guaranteeing my victory over all the works of the enemy. Jesus spoiled principalities and powers and made a show of them openly (Colossians 2:15). I am delivered from the power of darkness and translated into the Kingdom of Christ. In Christ, I have redemption through His Blood even the forgiveness of sins (Colossians 1:13, 14). For this very purpose Jesus came, that He might destroy the works of the devil (1 John 3:8). Now, sin has no dominion over me.

Thank You, Father, I am free indeed. Thank You, Father, for the cleansing power of the Blood. Christ, who through the eternal spirit offered Himself without spot to God, purges by His Blood my conscience from dead works, guilt, and condemnation so that I am able to serve and minister to God (Hebrews 9:14), in righteousness and truth having a pure conscience undefiled before God (Acts 24:16). Thank You, Father, that I have overcome the devil by the Blood of the Lamb, the Word of my testimony, and I love not my life even to death (Revelation 12:11). The Blood of Jesus symbolizes the obedience of Christ even to death. Wherefore God has highly exalted Jesus and given Him a name, which is supreme to every name. At the name of Jesus, every knee bows of things in Heaven, things in the earth, and things under the earth (Philippians 2:8-10). All power in Heaven and earth is in the name of Jesus (Matthew 28:18). The name of Jesus belongs to me and I am an overcomer.

Thank You, Father, for the authority I have as a believer in the name of Jesus, all because of the Blood of Christ. Because of the obedience of Christ as signified in His shed Blood, I have authority to tread on serpents and scorpions and nothing shall by any means hurt me (Luke 10:19). I have been given the keys of the Kingdom of Heaven, and whatever I bind on earth shall be bound in Heaven, and whatever I loosen on earth shall be loosened in Heaven (Matthew 18:19). Thank You, Father, for the Blood of Christ because it is the assurance of Your unconditional love for me. While I was yet a sinner, Christ died for me (Romans 5:8).

Thank You, Jesus, for loving me and washing me from my sins in Your own Blood. Thank You for making me a king and a priest unto God Your Father. To You be glory and dominion forever and ever, amen (Revelation 1:5-6). Finally, I thank You, Father, for my new life, my new hope, my new identity, and my new family all because of the Blood. I can never repay You for the price paid for my freedom, but I will always be thankful and let the love of Christ constrain me. I believe if one died for all, then all died. Jesus died for all, that I who live should live no longer for myself but for Jesus Who died for me and rose again (2 Corinthians 5:14,15). I am bought with a price. I belong to You Father God. I am sanctified and separated unto You, for Your purpose. I will glorify You in my body and my spirit which is Yours (1 Corinthians 6:20).

I will honour the Blood and be thankful by walking in fellowship and communion with the Blood of Christ (1 Corinthians 10:16). The consecration of my God is upon my head all the days of my life. I am holy unto the Lord (Numbers 6:7, 8). I honour the Blood by walking in the fear of the Lord, obedience, love, and faith. May the God of peace, that brought again from the dead my Lord Jesus, the great Shepherd of the sheep, through the Blood of the everlasting covenant make me perfect in every good work to do His will working in me that which is well pleasing in His sight through Jesus Christ to whom be glory forever and ever, amen (Hebrews 13:20, 21).

Section II: *Confessions*

C. My Walk with God

"Can two walk together, unless they are agreed?" (Amos 3:3)

Do All in Jesus' Name

"Whatsoever you do in word or in deed, do all in the Name of Jesus" (Colossians 3:17).

Live everyday in the name of Jesus. In every situation and every occasion, endeavour to present everything that Jesus is. All that is in Jesus is in His name. Allow Him to be your strength, your hope, and your righteousness. Take hold of Jesus through His name and face every obstacle with courage.

Let His love in you rise up and give you victory over fears, resentments, rejections, and disappointments. **"Whom the Son sets free is free indeed"** (John 8:36). Invoke the power of the name of Jesus, which is above every name, and let Jesus' name bring healing and wholeness to you.

Live Right, Do Right

Let me exhort you and challenge you from the Word of God and especially from the book of Titus.

You were not saved by virtue of any good deeds or moral achievements on your part. God, in His loving-kindness and through His tender mercies saved you by the cleansing power of the new birth and the renewing power of the Holy Spirit (Titus 3:4, 5). By grace you have been saved through faith. It is not your own doing; it is the gift of God (Ephesians 2:8).

Now that you are saved, God your Father expects you to be conformed to the character of Christ. He expects you to live in a manner that will bring glory to His Name. You are to renounce worldly passions and live sober, upright, and godly lives in this world. You are to live a responsible, honorable, and God-fearing life (Titus 2:12).

You are to do all that you have to do without grumbling and complaining. You are to be blameless and innocent, children of God without blemish in the midst of a crooked and perverse generation. You are to shine forth as lights in this world (Philippians 2:14, 15). You are the children of Light.

In addition, you are to be zealous for good works and eager to do good (Titus 2:14). Show mercy to others even as you have received mercy. Do not be judgmental or harsh, but treat others better than they deserve. You must demonstrate the love of God in word and in deed. Take opportunities that come along to do good and be rich in good works. The Bible says, when you show kindness, mercy, and love you are demonstrating that you are indeed a child of God (Matthew 5:45).

Come up Higher

I have been observing what the Lord has been doing, and discerning what the Spirit of God is saying to the church. I believe the Lord is calling the church to come up higher (Revelation 4:1), and be conformed to the overcoming, victorious Spirit of Christ that He has placed in us. You have been delivered from the authority of the devil. You have been born again by the Spirit of God. God's divine nature impregnates you. You were made in the image of God. You are His workmanship designed for greatness. God has fashioned you to rule and reign as a king or queen through Christ (Romans 5:17).

With Jesus as your Head and Master, you are to have

dominion over all the works of the devil. God's will is for you to prosper in every area of your life and be in health, even as your soul prospers (3 John 2). How much victory you enjoy and demonstrate is dependent on how much your soul prospers. How much your soul prospers is in proportion to how much your thinking and attitude becomes conformed to the mind of Christ (Romans 12:2; Romans 8:29).

"As a man thinks in his heart so is he" (Proverbs 23:7). It is said, your attitude determines your altitude. God wants you to have a sober, a vigilant, and a violent mindset against the enemy (1 Peter 5:8; Matthew 11:12). God wants you to have a humble and a contrite heart to His Word and Spirit (Psalm 51:17). You are to walk in obedience and abound with thanksgiving toward Him (Colossians 2:7).

You are to love God by loving and serving each other as you would the Lord, with all your heart and soul (Matthew 22:37-39). The spirit of excellence needs to permeate you so that whatever you do you may do it heartily as to the Lord and not as unto men (Colossians 3:23). The whole spirit of your mind must be renewed (Ephesians 4:23), so that you may walk in the spirit of victory that God has placed in you. Let the Lord stir up the spirit of victory in you today (1 Timothy 1:6). Bless the Lord and receive His Word today with joy and understanding.

My Christian Walk
(Based on scriptures that speak about 'always' and 'never')

"I have set the Lord always before me. Because He is at my right hand I shall not be moved" (Psalm 16:8). "Men ought always to pray" (Luke 18:1). "Taking the sword of the Spirit, *which is the word of God: praying always with all manner of prayers and supplication in the Spirit"* (Ephesians 6:17). I will *"pray without ceasing"* (1 Thessalonians 5:17), and *"rejoice in the Lord always"* (Philippians 4:4). I will *"rejoice evermore"* (1 Thessalonians 5:16), and bless the Lord at all times letting His praise continually be upon my lips (Psalm 34:1). In everything I give thanks, for this is the will of God in Christ Jesus concerning me (1 Thessalonians 5:18). I will meditate upon the Word day and night (Joshua 1:8). I will attend to His Words and incline my ear unto His sayings. I will not let them depart from my eyes, I will keep them in the midst of my heart. For they are life unto those who find them and health to all their flesh.

"I will keep my heart with all diligence for out of it are the issues of life" (Proverbs 4:20-23). I will be mindful always of His covenant (1 Chronicles 16:15), and be in the fear of the Lord all the day long (Proverbs 23:17).

I am a doer of the word, and not a hearer only (James 1:22). I always acknowledge the Lord in all my ways (Proverbs 3:5). I look unto Jesus, the Author and Finisher of my faith (Hebrews 12:2). I am just and I live by my faith (Romans 1:17).

I walk by faith not by sight (2 Corinthians 5:7). I look not at the things which are seen, but at the things which are not seen...the things which are eternal (2 Corinthians 4:18). My conversation is in Heaven (Philippians 3:20). I have a *better and enduring substance in Heaven (Hebrews 10:34).* *"Faith is the substance (and confidence) of things hoped for; the evidence I have of things not seen"* (Hebrews 11:1). I hold fast the profession and confession of my faith without wavering, because He is faithful that promised (Hebrews

10:23). His Word is forever settled in Heaven (Psalm 119:89), and He watches over His Word to perform it (Jeremiah 1:12).

Whatsoever is born of God overcomes the world, and this is the victory that overcomes the world, even my faith (1 John 5:4). I therefore continue steadfast in faith, always abounding in the work of the Lord, knowing that my labour is not in vain in the Lord (1 Corinthians 15:58). I earnestly contend for the faith (Jude 3). I fight the good fight of faith, laying hold on eternal life (1 Timothy 6:12). This is life eternal, that I may know Him, the only true God and Jesus Christ whom you have sent (John 17:3), and the power of His resurrection and the fellowship of His suffering being made conformable unto His death (Philippians 3:10). I am ready always to give and to distribute (Hebrews 13:16).

I reckon myself to be dead unto sin, but alive unto God through Jesus Christ my Lord (Romans 6:11). I give no place to the devil (Ephesians 4:27). I make no provision for the flesh (Romans 13:14). If I am angry, I sin not (Ephesians 4:26). I let no corrupt communication come out of my mouth (Ephesians 4:29). I am anxious for nothing, but in everything by prayer and supplication with thanksgiving, I let my requests be made known unto God. And the peace of God that passes all understanding keeps my heart and mind through Christ Jesus (Philippians 4:6-7). I am always bearing about in my body the dying of the Lord Jesus, that the life also of Jesus might be made manifest in my body (2 Corinthians 4:10).

"I forget those things which are behind, and reach forth unto those things which are before. I press toward the mark for the prize of the high calling of God in Christ Jesus" (Philippians 3:13,14). I labour fervently in prayer for myself and others, that we may all stand perfect and complete in the will of God (Colossians 4:12). I quench not the Spirit of God (2 Thessalonians 5:19), and grieve not the Holy Spirit whereby I am sealed unto the day of redemption (Ephesians 4:30). I have no fellowship with the unfruitful works of darkness, but rather I reprove them (Ephesians 5:11).

I stand fast in the liberty with which Christ has made me free, and I am not entangled with any yoke of bondage (Galatians 5:1). I will not be drunk with wine wherein is excess (Ephesians 5:18). *"All things are lawful for me, but all things are not expedient: all things are lawful for me, but all things edify not"* (1 Corinthians 10:23). I am continually filled with the Spirit (Ephesians 5:18). I am building up myself and my faith by praying in the Holy Ghost. I am keeping myself in the love of God (Jude 20:4), and unspotted from the world (James 1:27). I am looking for the mercy of my Lord Jesus Christ unto eternal life (Jude 21).

I trust in the Lord with all my heart (Proverbs 3:5) at all times (Psalm 34:1). I speak to myself in psalms, and hymns, and spiritual songs, singing and making melody in my heart to the Lord. I give thanks always for all things unto God, and the Father in the name of my Lord Jesus Christ (Ephesians 5:19-20).

Now unto Him who is able to keep me from falling, and to present me faultless before the presence of His glory with exceeding joy, to the only wise God our Saviour, be glory and majesty, dominion and power, both now and ever. Amen (Jude 24-25).

Being Led By The Spirit

My success in this life is determined by my following the

leading of the Holy Spirit. The Holy Spirit teaches me to profit and to be successful. He leads me in the way that I should go (Isaiah 48:17). The Spirit of God guides me into all truth (John 16:13).

It is my deepest desire to follow the leading of the Spirit every moment of the day in every area of my life. The Father is glorified and honoured when my life reflects His character, and is fruitful and successful (John 16:14; John 15:8). It is my Father's desire that I prosper in every area (3 John 2). He delights in my prosperity and success (Psalm 35:27). It gives my Father great joy when I walk in truth (3 John 4).

I realize I have enemies to my walk in the Spirit. My flesh and the carnal mind will oppose me (Romans 8:7). Nevertheless, the Spirit of God leads me in a manner to mortify the deeds of my body so that I have victory over the flesh (Romans 8:13). I am determined to be spiritually minded (Romans 8:6). I set my thoughts and affections on godly things (Colossians 3:2).

I refuse to be carnally minded. I live in the conscious awareness that I am a spirit and the Spirit of Truth dwells in my spirit (Ephesians 3:16). I know that the unseen (spirit) world is real. I am not ignorant of the spirit world (1 Corinthians 12:1), nor do I ignore the things of the Spirit.

I realize that as I am filled with and controlled by the Spirit of God, it is easier for me to recognize and follow the Spirit's leading (Luke 4:1). I am determined, therefore, to continually be filled with the Spirit (Ephesians 5:18). I practice the presence of God by maintaining a lifestyle of prayer, praise, and purity.

The Spirit of God confirms my inward convictions of the truth (Romans 8:16). I maintain a pure conscience (1 Timothy 1:19). I am alert to recognize the still small voice of the Holy Spirit speaking to my spirit. I walk in faith, love, and righteousness (Isaiah 32:17). I expect the peace of God to be manifested in every decision I need to make and decide with finality every matter that arises in my mind (Colossians 3:15).

No longer will I ever say I do not hear God's voice. I am learning to recognize the voice of my Master more and more each day. The voice of a stranger I will not follow. I know my Master's voice and I follow Him (John 10:3-5).

My Conscience

Bodily exercise profits little, but godliness is profitable unto all things, having promise of the life that now is and of that which is to come (1 Timothy 4:8). I therefore purpose in my heart to exercise myself to always have a conscience void of offense toward God and toward men (Acts 24:16) by renouncing the hidden things of dishonesty, not walking in craftiness, nor handling the Word of God deceitfully, but by manifestation of the truth commending myself to every man's conscience in the sight of God (2 Corinthians 4:2). I speak the truth in Christ, my conscience bearing me witness in the Holy Ghost (Romans 9:1). For my conscience gives testimony accusing or else excusing me (2 Corinthians 1:12; Romans 2:15).

If my heart and conscience condemn me not, then I have confidence towards God. And whatsoever I ask I receive of Him, because I keep His commandments, and do those things that are pleasing in His sight (1 John 3:21,22). I therefore live in all good conscience before God (Acts 23:1), in whose sight all things are naked and opened unto the eyes of Him with whom I have to do (Hebrews 4:13). God is a Spirit, and they that worship and serve Him must worship and serve Him in Spirit and in Truth (John 4:24).

Now the end of the commandment is love out of a pure heart and a good conscience, and faith that is sincere (1 Timothy 1:5). I will fight the good fight of faith (1 Timothy 6:12), armed not only with faith, but with a clear, pure, wholesome conscience, which some have sadly put away (1 Timothy 1:19). I will always remember to hold the mystery of faith in a pure conscious (1 Timothy 3:9). *"I sanctify the Lord God in my heart with meekness and fear, having a good conscience, that whereas they speak evil of me, as of evildoers, they may be ashamed that falsely accuse my good conversation in Christ"* (1 Peter 3:15,16). I honour all men, love the brotherhood, and fear God (1 Peter 2:17). I remember them which have the rule over me (Hebrews 13:7). I believe the best of every person (1 Corinthians 13:7). Unto the pure all things are pure, but unto them that are defiled and unbelieving is nothing pure, but even their mind and conscience is defiled (Titus 1:15).

I let my heart be established with grace not meat (Hebrews 13:9). *"For the kingdom of God is not meat and drink; but righteousness, peace, and joy in the Holy Ghost"* (Romans 14:17). If for a good conscience toward God I endure grief, suffering wrongfully, I take it patiently, this is acceptable to God (I Peter 2:19,20) Who is able to make all grace abound toward me (II Corinthians 9:8), that I may abound in hope through the power of the Holy Ghost (Romans 15:13). Now unto him that knows to do good, and does it not, to him it is sin (James 4:1). I walk therefore in the light as He is the light and the blood of Jesus Christ His Son cleanses me from all sin (1 John 1:7). Jesus, Who through the eternal Spirit offered Himself without spot to God, by His blood, is able to purge my conscience from dead works to serve the living God (Hebrews 9:14), so that I, as a worshipper, once purged, should have no more conscience of sin (Hebrews 10:2). I draw near with a true heart in full assurance of faith, having my heart sprinkled from an evil conscience and my body washed with pure water (Hebrews 10:22).

Diligence—Part 1

Father God, Your Word declares that Your *"eyes are over the righteous, and Your ears are open to their prayers"* (I Peter 3:12). Jesus also declared that He chose me, and ordained me that I should bring forth fruit, and that my fruit should remain, that whatever I ask You Father in His name You may give me (John 15:16). Father, in the name of Jesus, I ask in faith for the spirit of diligence in my life and ministry, so that I bear much fruit and that You may be glorified (John 15:8). I receive Your grace to keep my heart with all diligence, for out of it are the issues of life (Proverbs 4:23).

I guard all the gateways to my heart with all diligence unless any root of bitterness springs up to trouble me, and by this I become defiled (Hebrews 12:15). I choose to walk circumspectly, not as a fool but as wise (Ephesians 5:15). I choose the fear of the Lord (Proverbs 1:29) that all my pathways be established in mercy and truth (Proverbs 4:26; Proverbs 3:3). I am diligent to be found by Him in peace, without spot and blameless (2 Peter 3:14). Lord, set a watch over my mouth, keep watch over the door of my lips (Psalm 141:3), that I sin not with my tongue. I will keep my mouth with a bridle, especially when the wicked are before me (Psalm 39:1). I will be wise and study to answer (Proverbs 15:28) and my heart will teach my mouth (Proverbs 16:23). I will be quick to hear and slow to speak (James 1:19). Father,

You have commanded me to keep Your precepts diligently (Psalm 119:4). Your commandment is exceedingly broad (Psalm 119:96). I esteem all Your precepts concerning all things to be right, and I hate every false way (Psalm 119:128).

I have determined that I will earnestly contend for the faith (Jude 3). I will diligently keep Your commandments. I will do that which is right and good in Your sight (Deuteronomy 6:17). I choose to make Your Word my meditation all the day long (Psalm 119:99). I will commune with my own heart upon my bed, and be still (Psalm 4:4). I will meditate within my heart, and my spirit will make diligent search in God (Psalm 77:6). I will hide Your Word in my heart, that I might not sin against You (Psalm 119:11). I will delight myself in Your statutes. I will not forget Your Word (Psalm 119:16). I will give attention to Your Word, and incline my ear to Your sayings. I will not let them depart from my eyes (Proverbs 4:20,21). They shall be as frontlets between my eyes. I will lay Your Words up in my heart and in my soul, and bind them for a sign upon my hand (Deuteronomy 11:18). The book of the Law will not depart out of my mouth (Joshua 1:8). I will hold fast to the confession of my faith without wavering (Hebrews 10:23). Jesus, You are the high priest of my confession (Hebrews 3:11) and You are faithful to watch over my words (Psalm 17:3), when they match Your words, to perform them (Jeremiah 1:12).

Father, I believe for the anointing of diligence to affect my prayer life: confessions, meditations, readings, studying, preaching, and serving. I commit to give myself continually to prayer and the ministry of the Word (Acts 6:4). I commit to be earnest in prayer and to be vigilant therein with thanksgiving (Colossians 4:2); always laboring earnestly for others and myself that we may stand perfect and complete in all Your will O Lord (Colossians 4:12).

I thank You, my God, that I speak with tongues (1 Corinthians 14:18). I am determined to diligently build myself up continually on my most holy faith, praying in the Holy Spirit (Jude 20). Jesus is my example and I will follow Him. *"In the morning Jesus rose up a long while before daylight, He went out and departed to a solitary place, and there He prayed"* (Mark 1:35). In the days of His flesh, when He had offered up prayers and supplications, with vehement cries and tears to Him Who was able to save Him from death, He was heard because of His godly fear (Hebrews 5:7). From the rising of the sun, I will call upon God (Psalm 55:16). You shall hear my voice in the morning, O Lord; in the morning I will direct my prayer to You, and I will look up (Psalm 5:3). I bring my body into subjection (1 Corinthians 9:27), to the obedience of Christ, the Anointed (2 Corinthians 10:5).

I will be diligent in the work of the ministry and the call of God to preach among the Gentiles the unsearchable riches of Christ and to make all men see what is the fellowship of the mystery (Ephesians 3:8,9). I thank You, Jesus, for enabling me, and counting me faithful, putting me into the ministry (2 Timothy 1:12). I am determined to walk worthy of You, Lord, unto all pleasing, making full proof of my ministry (1 Timothy 4:5), being zealous of good works (Titus 2:14) and waging the good warfare (1 Timothy 1:18). My meat is to do the will of Him who sent me, and to finish the work my Father has given me (John 4:34).

I rest in the fullness of faith (Hebrews 10:22) holding the mystery of faith with a pure conscience (1 Timothy 3:9). My Father has been working until now, and I have been working (John 5:17). Father, You dwell in me and You do the works (John 14:10). I labour to enter into Your rest

(Hebrews 4:11). I rest in Your Anointing and Your Anointed. I refuse to fall short by unbelief (Hebrews 4:1). I am a worker with Christ (2 Corinthians 6:1) and heirs together with the saints of the grace of life (1 Peter 3:7). I will be watchful with all perseverance and supplication for all saints (Ephesians 6:18), being diligent to know the state of the flocks and looking well to the herds (Proverbs 27:23). *"Besides all these things I will diligently add to my faith virtue, and to virtue knowledge, and to knowledge temperance, and to temperance patience, and to patience godliness, and to godliness brotherly kindness, and to brotherly kindness love"* (2 Peter 1:5-7).

I believe You, Father, for the fruits of the righteousness of diligence to be increased in my life (2 Corinthians 9:10). As these fruits be in me and abound, I will neither be barren nor unfruitful in the revelation knowledge of my Lord Jesus Christ (2 Peter 1:5-8). I have great peace because I love Your law, and nothing shall offend me (Psalm 119:65). Grace and peace are multiplied to me through the increased knowledge of God and of Jesus my Lord (2 Peter 1:2). God bless me with every spiritual blessing there is in Heavenly places in Christ the anointed (Ephesians 1:3). *"The diligent soul shall be made fat"* (Proverbs 13:4). Isaiah 10:27 says: *"The yoke will be broken because of the anointing."* Diligence in God causes increase and multiplication in His anointing, and I am able to show myself strong and bring great things to pass as I diligently obey Your voice O Lord (Zechariah 6:15). The substance of a diligent man is precious (Proverbs 12:27). The hand of the diligent makes rich (Proverbs 10:4), and the hand of the diligent shall rule (Proverbs 12:24). The plans of the diligent lead surely to plenty (Proverbs 21:5). I am diligent and I excel in my work. I will stand before kings (Proverbs 22:29). The blessing of the Lord makes me rich, and He adds no sorrow with it (Proverbs 10:22).

It shall come to pass, when I diligently obey the voice of the Lord my God, to observe and to do all His commandments, the Lord my God will set me high above all nations of the earth, and all these blessings will come on me and overtake me (Deuteronomy 28:1-2). The blessings of Abraham shall come upon me through Christ Jesus (Galatians 3:14). I shall be blessed in the city and blessed in the field (Deuteronomy 28:3). The Lord shall command the blessing upon me (Deuteronomy 28:8).

The Lord shall establish me that I may go in and possess the good land which the Lord swore to give (Deuteronomy 6:18). Every place the sole of my feet shall tread upon, He will give to me (Deuteronomy 11:14), and even the heathen for my inheritance and the uttermost parts of the earth for my possession (Psalm 2:8). The Lord will give me great and beautiful cities which I did not build, and houses full of all good things, which I did not fill (Deuteronomy 6:10-11). I set my heart therefore to show diligence to the full assurance of hope to the end that I do not become slothful, but be a follower of them who through faith and patience inherit the promises (Hebrews 6:11-12), lest Satan should get an advantage of me, for I am not ignorant of his devices (2 Corinthians 2:11). I declare that I am delivered and free from slothfulness, procrastination, lukewarmness, complacency, and compromise. I have the victory through my Lord Jesus Christ (1 Corinthians 15:57). I therefore exercise my will to be steadfast, unmovable, always abounding in the work of the Lord. I know that my labour is not in vain in the Lord (1 Corinthians 15:58). The diligent soul shall be satisfied with fatness (Proverbs 13:4). Diligence is my doorway to understanding the fear of God (Proverbs 2:1-5). I am diligent to make my call and election sure, for if I do these things I will never stumble, but rather an entrance will be supplied to me abundantly into the everlasting kingdom of my Lord and Saviour Jesus Christ (2 Peter 1:10-11).

Diligence—Part 2

Father God, Your Word declares that Your eyes are over the righteous, and Your ears are open to their prayers (1 Peter 3:12). Father, in Jesus' name, I ask in faith for a spirit of diligence in my life, so that I may bear much fruit and that You would be glorified (John 15:8).

Out of my heart flows the issues of life (Proverbs 4:23). I will therefore guard all the gateways of my heart with great diligence and not allow any root of bitterness, unforgiveness, resentment, envy, or offence to spring up and quench the grace of God in my life (Hebrews 12:15). I am diligent to be found in peace without spot and blameless (2 Peter 3:14).

I give Your Word first place and make it a top priority in my life. I will hide Your Word in my heart that I might not sin against You (Psalm 119:11). I will give attention to Your Word, and incline my ear to Your sayings. I will not let them depart from my eyes (Proverbs 4:20-21). Your Word is my meditation all the day long (Psalm 119:99).

Life and death is in the power of my tongue (Proverbs 18:21). A wholesome tongue is a tree of life (Proverbs 15:4). I refuse to be snared by the words of my mouth (Proverbs 6:2). I will not give the devil any place in my life, family, or affairs by negative, critical, fear-filled confessions or murmurings (1Corinthians 10:10; Matthew 15:11). The Word of God shall not depart from my mouth (Joshua 1:8). I overcome the enemy by the faith filled words of my Father

(Revelation 12:11; Proverbs 12:6). Lord, set a watch over my mouth, and keep watch over the door of my lips (Psalm 141:3), that I do not sin with my tongue. I will keep my mouth with a bridle (Psalm 39:1). I will be quick to hear and slow to speak (James 1:19).

Father God, I believe to walk in diligence in my prayer life, always labouring earnestly for others and myself that we may stand perfect and complete in the will of God (Colossians 4:12). The diligent soul shall be made fat (Proverbs 13:4). The hand of the diligent shall rule (Proverbs 12:24).

My Walk with God

How can two walk together except they are agreed? (Amos 3:3). I am in agreement with God (1 John 1:3).

The Spirit of God is Holy and He is love (Romans 5:3). I choose therefore to walk in love and holiness.

God is a faith God. I am His child and I have His nature. I walk by faith and not by sight (2 Corinthians 5:7), *"for without faith it is impossible to please Him"* (Hebrews 11:6).

God is one with His Word (John 1:1). I believe the Word above all else. I exalt the Word above circumstances and the reasoning of men (Romans 3:4). The Word of God is the final authority in every matter in my life (Psalm 138:2; Psalm 119:89). My thoughts, my actions, and even my emotions are ordered by the Word of God (2 Corinthians 10:5; James 1:21). God is a Spirit (John 4:24). I am born of God and I am one spirit with Him (1 Corinthians 6:17). I live a fasting lifestyle that I may be more sensitive to the Spirit of God, and to Spiritual realities (Joel 2:12; Matthew 17:21). In addition, I set my heart and will to pray often and habitually in other tongues, that I may be built up in my spirit by the Spirit of God (1 Corinthians 14:2), and be receptive to the Spirit of revelation, wisdom, understanding, council, might, knowledge and the fear of the Lord (Isaiah 11:2-3).

God reserves intimate fellowship for them that fear Him (Psalm 4:3; Psalm 25:14). I choose the fear of the Lord (Proverbs 1:29). I hate evil, pride, sin and iniquity (Proverbs 8:13). I love righteousness, justice, humility, mercy, and truth. Father, I receive Your all sufficient grace (II Corinthians 12:9), to walk in these things by the power of Your Spirit, in Jesus' name!

God, My Father

God is my Father. I am His child. I am a new creation born of His Spirit. I am a partaker of His nature—Eternal Life. The Blood of Jesus, the Word of God, and the witness of the Holy Spirit give me absolute assurance of my relationship with Him. The Father loves me even as He loves Jesus.

I have the legal right to use the name of Jesus. All authority in Heaven and earth is wrapped up in the name of Jesus. Jesus defeated Satan on my behalf. I have authority over all the power of the enemy in Jesus' name. I have in me the same spirit that raised Jesus from the dead. I have the same righteousness that Jesus had, for He Himself is my righteousness. The works that Jesus did I will do also, and greater works. I can come in confidence, at any time before my Father's throne of grace. Whatsoever I ask of my Father in Jesus' name, He will give it to me. I am being firmly established in the thrilling reality that God is my Father indeed, and I am His child and heir. Praise the Lord!

(1 John 3:1-2; 2 Corinthians 5:17; 1 Corinthians 6:17; 2 Peter 1:4; 1 John 5:7-9; John 17:23; John 16:23; Matthew 28:18; Colossians 2:15; Luke 10:19; Romans 8:11; 1 Corinthians 1:30; John 14:12; Hebrews 4:16).

Section II: *Confessions*

D. Victorious Living

But thanks be to God, who gives us the victory through our Lord Jesus Christ"
(1 Corinthians 15:57).

Overcomers

"Let him who has ears to hear, hear what the Spirit says unto the churches: To him that overcomes I will give to eat of the tree of life, which is in the midst of the Paradise of God" (Revelation 2:7). *"Be faithful unto death, and I will give you the crown of life"* (Revelation 2:10). *"He who overcomes shall not be hurt with the second death"* (Revelation 2:11). *"To him who overcomes I will give to eat of the hidden manna. And I will give him a white stone, and on the stone a new name written which no man knows except he who receives it"* (Revelation 2:17). *"He who overcomes, and keeps my works until the end, to him I will give power over the nations. He shall rule them with a rod of iron as the vessels of a potter shall they be broken to shivers, even as I also received of my Father; and I will give him the morning star"* (Revelation 2:26-28). *"He who overcomes shall be clothed in white raiment, and I will not blot out his name from the Book of life; but I will confess his name before my Father and before His angels"* (Revelation 3:5). *"He who overcomes, I will make him a pillar in the temple of My God, and he shall go out no more. I will write on him the name of My God and the name of the city of My God, the New Jerusalem which comes down out of heaven from My God. And I will write on him My new name"* (Revelation 3:12). *"To him who overcomes I will grant to sit with Me on My throne, as I also overcame and sat down with My Father on His throne"* (Revelation 3:21).

"I write to you, young men, because you are strong, and the word of God abides in you, and you have overcome the wicked one" (1 John 2:14). *"Whatever is born of God overcomes the world. And this is the victory that has overcome the world—even our faith"* (I John 5:4). *"You are of God, little children, and have overcome them, because He who is in you is greater

than he who is in the world" (1 John 4:4). *"In the world you shall have tribulation; but be of good cheer. I have overcome the world"* (John 16:33). *"For this purpose the Son of God was manifested, that He might destroy the works of the devil"* (I John 3:1). *"They overcame him by the blood of the Lamb and by the word of their testimony, and they did not love their lives to the death"* (Revelation 12:11). *"I am the Alpha and Omega, the Beginning and the End. I will give of the fountain of the water of life freely to him who thirsts. He who overcomes shall inherit all things. and I will be his God, and he shall be My son"* (Revelation 21:6-7).

In all these things we are more than conquerors through Him who loved us (Romans 8:37). The Lamb shall overcome the enemy, for He is the Lord of Lords and King of Kings; and those who are with Him are called, chosen, and faithful (Revelation 17:14).

The Fight of Faith

In the fight of faith, my weapon is the sword of the spirit that is the Word of God (Ephesians 6:16-17). My battle is with reason, which is governed by the information coming through my senses. When sense knowledge goes beyond what it sees, feels, and hears, it goes into the realm of speculation, theory, and hypothesis. Faith deals with Truth. The Word of God has no speculation or theories, just declarations of facts. My faith does not stand in the wisdom of men (sense knowledge) but rather in the power of God— The Word (1 Corinthians 2:5). By the Word of God, the heavens were created (Psalm 33:6). No Word of God is void of power (Luke 1:37).

I know who I am in Christ, Hell fears me and Heaven rejoices. When I step into selfishness, I break fellowship with love, and therefore with God, since God is love, and I give place to the enemy (Ephesians 4:27). Regardless of how many promises I plead if I do not walk in love my prayer life will be a failure (Mark 11:25). If I walk in love (my heart knows if I am practicing love toward men), I can walk into the Father's presence as Jesus did in confidence, and know that my prayers will be answered (1 John 3:21-22).

This Is What I Believe

I have eternal life. In Jesus' name I cast out devils. I lay hands on the sick and they recover. If I drink any deadly thing, it shall by no means hurt me. Signs and wonders follow me. The works that Jesus did, I do also. I can do all things through Christ who strengthens me. I am who God said I am. I can do what God says I can do. I have what God says I have. I have the mind of Christ. Nothing is impossible to me as a believer. All things are possible to me. Me and my entire household shall be saved. I am anointed by the Spirit of God to preach, teach, heal, and establish believers in Christ. The power of God is upon me. I am His sheep and I hear His voice, and a voice of a stranger I will not follow. God speaks to me through His Son by His Spirit. Jesus is the way; I cannot be lost. Jesus is the truth; I shall not be deceived. Jesus is the life; I shall never die. The glory of God is in me. All my bills are paid, and I have more than enough to abound to every good work. I am blessed going in, and I am blessed going out. Out of my belly flows rivers of living water. I am in God's kingdom, and I am free from the works of darkness. In Christ, I am the light of the world and the salt of the earth. I am a believer; I am not a doubter. I am the righteousness of God in Christ. I am one with God. The life that I now live, is the life of Christ. My old life is gone forever. I have the right to use the name of Jesus as my own. I am bold as a lion. The power of God is ever increasing in my life.

(John 5:24; Mark 16:17,18; John 14:12; Philippians 4:13; 1 Corinthians 2:16; Mark 9:23; Acts 16:31; 2 Corinthians 1:21; John 10:4,5; John 14:6; John 11:26; Colossians 1:27; Philippians 4:19; 2 Corinthians 9:8; Deuteronomy 28:6; John 7:38; Colossians 1:13; Matthew 5:13,14; 2 Corinthians 5:21; 1 Corinthians 6:17; Galatians 2:20; Colossians 3:17; Proverbs 28:1)

The Spirit of Victory

I have the Spirit of Christ in me (Romans 8:9). The Spirit of Christ is a Spirit of total victory. I know no failure. I know no defeat, because the Spirit of Christ dwells in me.

I am made in the image of my Heavenly Father. I am created in righteousness and true holiness (Ephesians 4:24). I am God's own handiwork (Ephesians 2:10). His nature impregnates me. My new spiritual nature is eternal life, the same as my Father. Through my Father all things are possible to me. I cannot be defeated. If God be for me what does it matter who may be against me (Romans 8:31).

Greater is He that is in me than he that is in the world (1 John 4:4). I am not being arrogant, puffed up, nor inflated with pride. In fact, I am humbling myself to the truth that the Lord is my strength and salvation, of whom shall I be afraid (Psalm 27:1). I am totally dependent on my omnipotent, omniscient, and omnipresent Father Who dwells in me. All things are possible to him that believes (Mark 9:23).

I am a believer not a doubter. All things are possible to me. I depend on the might of the Spirit of God that is in me. *"I can do all things through Christ who strengtheneth me"*

(Philippians 4:13).

I am one with the Father in Christ. Christ is made to me righteousness. As a child of God I have rights and privileges. I am a joint heir with Christ and an heir of God unto all things (Romans 8:17; Hebrews 1:2). All things are mine (1 Corinthians 3:21). I am blessed with every spiritual blessing in heavenly places in Christ (Ephesians 1:3). God has given to me all things that pertain to life and godliness (2 Peter 1:3).

The devil is my Father's enemy and my enemy. I am not ignorant of the devil's tricks (2 Corinthians 2:11). I am sober and vigilant (1 Peter 5:8). I give the devil no place in my life (Ephesians 4:27) through sin, pride, or unbelief. I make no provisions for the flesh (Romans 13:14). I put on the armour of light (Romans 13:12). I put on the Lord Jesus Christ (Romans 13:14). I clothe myself with humility (1 Peter 5:5). I submit to God and resist the devil, and he flees from me (James 4:7).

In the name of Jesus I have authority over the devil and all his works (Luke 10:19). I operate in a spirit of violence against the enemy (Matthew 11:12). I cast down every imagination and pull down every barrier that erects itself against the knowledge of God. I compel every thought to surrender in obedience to the authority of Christ (2 Corinthians 10:5). I walk in love so that there is nothing in me to cause me to stumble (1 John 2:10). I overcome the devil by the Blood of the Lamb and the Word of my testimony (Romans 12:11).

I abound in thanksgiving towards God (Colossians 2:7). In everything I give thanks (1 Thessalonians 5:18). *"Thanks to*

God who always causes me to triumph in Christ" (2 Corinthians 2:14). I am victorious in Christ. I have the spirit of faith. I believe and therefore I speak (2 Corinthians 4:13). I meditate on God's Word day and night (Joshua 1:8). I give myself wholly to the Word (1 Timothy 4:15). I magnify the Word above everything (Psalm 138:2). My delight is in the Word (Psalm 1:2). I meditate in the Word until I can see in my heart what the Lord is saying to me (Habakkuk 2:1). I meditate in the Word until light, revelation, wisdom, and understanding erupts on the inside of me (2 Peter 1:19). When I see it in my heart, I believe and decree it and it shall come to pass (Job 22:28). I meditate in the Word until it becomes *Rhema* to me. When the Word through meditation becomes spirit and life in me (John 6:63), I can say to this mountain be removed to another place and it shall remove and nothing shall be impossible to me (Matthew 17:20).

There is a three-fold victory cord (Ecclesiastes 4:12) that the enemy cannot defeat because each cord is of God (1 John 5:4). The Word, the Spirit, and the Blood make a three-fold cord (1 John 5:8). That three-fold cord is my vehicle to personal victory:

- I walk in the Word through meditation.
- I walk in the Spirit through praying without ceasing.
- I walk in the Blood through holiness.

I cannot be defeated in Christ. Thanks be to God who gives me the victory through the Lord Jesus Christ (1 Corinthians 15:57).

I Refuse to Fear

I will not fear because I have favour with God (Luke 1:30). The Lord God Almighty is on my side (Psalm 118:6). In these last days, when the spirit of terror runs wild, my heart will not fail me because of fear (Luke 21:26). I am established in righteousness (Isaiah 54:14). I know in whom I have believed, and I am persuaded that God is able to keep me and that which I have committed to Him (2 Timothy 1:12). Oppression and terror will be far from me because I will not permit fear in my life (Isaiah 54:14).

Christ, my Redeemer, has destroyed the enemy that had the power of death, and He has delivered me from being held in bondage through the fear of death (Hebrews 2:14-15). The law of sin, death and fear is no longer dominating my life. The law of the Spirit of Life in Christ Jesus now rules my life (Romans 8:2). I am completely redeemed from fear (Galatians 3:13).

Fear uses weakness and ignorance to access my life. I am not weak. I am strong in the Lord and in the power of His might (Ephesians 6:10). I am not ignorant (2 Corinthians 2:11). I am taught of the Lord and great is my peace (Isaiah 54:13).

I know God's favour. The Lord is gracious, full of compassion, slow to anger and of great mercy (Psalm 145:8). The mountains may depart and the hills may be removed, but the lovingkindness of the Lord shall never depart from me (Isaiah 54:10). The Lord is my helper, and He will never leave me nor forsake me (Hebrews 12:6,5). I will not fear. I know the love of Christ which passes all knowledge (Ephesians 3:19). The Father loves me as dearly as He loves Jesus (John 17:23). The knowledge of God's love banishes fear from my life (1 John 4:18). God has a good plan for my life (Jeremiah 29:11). I will not fear.

I know and believe God's Word and promises. I have a joy and peace that comes from believing so that I am able to abound in hope through the power of the Holy Spirit (Romans 15:13). If fear attempts to enter my heart I will resist it (James 4:7), and I will run to the rock that is higher than I (Psalm 61:2). I will take my refuge in God. I refuse to fear. I have a sound mind (2 Timothy 1:7). I will cast down every fearful thought that exalts itself against the knowledge of God (2 Corinthians 10:5). I am strong and very courageous for the Lord is with me (Joshua 1:9). No weapon formed against me will prosper (Isaiah 54:17).

My eyes are not fixed on the circumstances (2 Corinthians 4:18). My eyes are fixed on Jesus and His Word. Jesus is the Author and Finisher of my faith (Hebrews 12:2). Jesus is the Captain of my salvation (Hebrews 2:10). I shall not fear.

Dear Friend, if you suffer from fear do the following:

1. Make these confessions out loud every day.
2. Carefully study these confession.

    a. Write down at least five things you **need to do.**
    b. Write down seven truths you **need to know.**

3. Choose at least one scripture to memorize.
4. Boldly confess memorized scripture at least ten times a day.

Reaping with Joy

Galatians 6:9 says, *"Let us not be weary in doing good, for in due season you shall reap; if you faint not."* Joy is a fruit of the Spirit that works as a force to strengthen you. *"The joy of the Lord is your strength"* (Nehemiah 8:10). Isaiah 9:3

speaks of the joy of harvest. Joel 1:12 says if your joy withers, your harvest will also dry up. Psalm 126:5 says, *"we sow in tears, but we shall reap in joy."* According to Isaiah 12:3, you can receive salvation, deliverance, wholeness, and your harvest using the force of joy as consciously and purposefully as one would draw water from a well with a bucket. Joy is your bucket.

James 1:2 says: *"Count it all joy when you fall into various trials and tests."*

Philippians 4:4 says: *"Rejoice in the Lord always."* If the devil can't steal your joy, he can't steal your stuff. So then, strengthen and guard your joy.

Joy comes from believing (Romans 15:13). Here are four ways to strengthen your joy:

1. Meditate and feed on God's Word (Jeremiah 15:16).
2. Rest in the truth that you are called by His name (Jeremiah 15:16), and that you are clothed with His righteousness (Isaiah 61:10).
3. Know God as Jehovah—"The Revealing One," your answer in every situation. Trust Him and don't be afraid (Isaiah 12:2).
4. Spend time in God's presence through praise and prayer (Psalm 16:11; Psalm 27:3).

Make this confession out loud: In nothing will I be terrified by the enemy (Philippians 1:28), but in the midst of trouble I will laugh (Job 5:22), and offer the sacrifices of joy (Psalm 27: 6). I will sing, shout, rejoice, and praise the name of the Lord (Isaiah 12:4-6; Psalm 32:11; Psalm 33:1). The Lord will give me strength and victory (Psalm 67:5,6).

Free from Shame

I am a new creation in Christ. I am a brand new man. Old things have passed away (2 Corinthians 5:17). I have been born again. I am more than a conqueror (Romans 8:37). That is who I am.

My future will not be determined by my past. How I was born, where I was born, the family and circumstances into which I was born shall not determine my future. In the name of Jesus I will not allow shame from the past to hinder my future. I forget those things which are behind and I reach out for those things that are ahead (Philippians 3:13). God has a good plan for my life (Jeremiah 29:11). My Father has good works and pathways planned for me to walk in (Ephesians 2:10). I will walk in these pathways and see God's plan for my life fulfilled.

God has deliberately chosen what the world calls foolish to shame the wise, and the weak things to shame the strong, and the things that the world counts poor and insignificant to overthrow and bring to nothing the things that exist (1 Corinthians 1:27-28). My responsibility is to present my body a living sacrifice, holy and acceptable to God (Romans 12:1). My responsibility is to have a broken and contrite heart before God, and to be renewed in the spirit of my mind (Psalm 51:17; Ephesians 4:23).

Dear Heavenly Father, I put away all pride and unbelief. I ask You O Lord to create in me a clean heart and a broken and contrite spirit (Psalm 51:10). Teach me to hate sin and to tremble at Your Word (Isaiah 66:2).

Melt me and mold me that I may be a vessel through which Your glory shines (Jeremiah 18:4; 2 Timothy 2:21). I am delivered and set free from the shame of the past by the

Blood of Christ (Isaiah 54:4-5).

Through repentance, humility and faith I step into the pathways of righteousness that You have prepared for me to walk in. In Jesus' name, I forgive the injustices committed against me. I release the hurts of the past and receive healing for the wounds inflicted on me. I will not nurse, curse or rehearse them anymore. I believe the Lord will reverse them. In the name of Jesus, I uproot resentment and bitterness from my life and cast them out (Hebrews 12:15). I give no place to the devil (Ephesians 4:27).

I choose to be a person of integrity. I keep my vows even when it may be inconvenient or hurtful to me (Psalm 15:4). Your Word promises me that because I walk in thanksgiving and keep my vows, if I call on You in the day of trouble You will deliver me (Psalm 50:14-15). Thank You, Lord, for continued deliverance and preservation.

My Soul Will Bless the Lord

Wise men worship God (Matthew 2:2,11). I will rejoice in the Lord and be glad. His praise shall continually be in my mouth. I will bless the Lord at all times. My soul, I am talking to you! We are going to bless the Lord. Soul, it does not matter what you feel like or what the circumstances say, we are going to bless the Lord. In fact, all that is within me, let us bless His Holy Name, right now. Praise the Lord! You are worthy to be praised, Oh, God! I bless your Holy name! Hallelujah! (Psalm 103:1; Psalm 34:1; Psalm 18:3).

Filled with His Fullness

I confess that I am being filled with the knowledge of God's will in all wisdom, and in all spiritual understanding. I am being filled with the fullness of God. I declare that the Spirit of the Lord is upon me, and He has anointed me to preach the gospel to the poor. He has sent me to heal the brokenhearted, to preach deliverance to the captives and the recovering of sight to the blind, to set at liberty them that are bruised, and to preach the acceptable year of the Lord and the day of vengeance of our God (Isaiah 61:1-2). I am filled with the Spirit of the Lord. I am filled with the Spirit of wisdom and understanding, with the Spirit of counsel and might, with the Spirit of knowledge and the fear of the Lord, which makes me of quick understanding in the fear of the Lord (Isaiah 11:2-3).

I am filled with power, joy, and faith. I rebuke and resist doubt, unbelief, disobedience, rebellion, and fear in the name of Jesus. I resist pride and arrogance. I am strong in faith, and I believe according to as "it is written". I am always giving glory to God knowing the love of God and the power of God, and knowing that God is able and is faithful and watches over His word to perform it (Jeremiah 1:12). To God be all the glory for He is ever mindful of His covenant (Psalm 111:5). The life I now live is the life of Christ, the Anointed (Galatians 2:20). I can do all things through Christ who strengthens me and makes me able. Christ is my sufficiency (2 Corinthians 3:5). All things are possible to me (Mark 9:23).

I totally yield my will to the Spirit of God. I live and breathe for the will of God. God is first, last and everything in my life. For me to live is Christ. In Him I live and move and have my being. All that I am, and all that I have, and all that is mine is Christ's. All that is Christ's is mine. I have a better covenant, based on better promises. I have a better priesthood, better sacrifices and better hope written in the blood of Jesus Christ, the Lamb of God, my Substitute, my

Lord, and my Master (Hebrews 7:11; Hebrews 9:22; Hebrews 8:6). I am running the way of God's commandments for He is enlarging my heart (Psalm 119:32). My feet shall not slip, for He enlarges my path under me (Psalm 18:36).

I am ever increasing in the knowledge of God and moving into perfection. I am full of the Holy Spirit, power, fire and the glory of the Lord. I am bold as a lion (Proverbs 28:1) and clothed with humility. My tongue is single, belonging only to God. I am a bondservant of the Lord Jesus Christ. I am determined to follow Him and obey Him always. Amen.

The Anointing In Me

Praise God! I am washed by the Blood of Jesus (Revelation 1:5). I am in love with Jesus, and He is in love with me. I am a new creation in the Anointed (2 Corinthians 5:17). My Father God has blessed me with every spiritual blessing in Heavenly places in the Anointed (Ephesians 1:3). I am crucified with the Anointed, and it is no longer I that live but the Anointed that lives in me (Galatians 2:20). The anointing is my life, my peace, my joy, my victory and my strength (Colossians 3:4). My omnipotent Father has called me to be an ambassador of the Anointed (2 Corinthians 5:20), and to show forth the praises of Him that has called me out of darkness into His marvelous light (1 Peter 2:9). I am commissioned to be a light in the world, and to manifest His glory (Matthew 5:16). As an apostle of Christ (2 Corinthians 3:3), I am determined to walk worthy of the Lord (Ephesians 4:1), and permeate my environment with the fragrance of His anointing and presence (2 Corinthians 2:14-16).

The Anointing lives in me and equips me for every task and calling in my life (1 John 1:27). I can do all things through the Anointing (Philippians 4:13). The anointing in me is Christ in me my hope and expectation of glory, victory, perfection and excellency (Colossians 1:27). I have not yet arrived, but I press on daily (Philippians 3:13-14). I count all things but loss that I may win Christ (Philippians 3:8). As I meditate upon Jesus and His Word, worship and praise Him, obey the voice of His Spirit, and walk in love, I am being changed from glory to glory by the power of His Spirit which is the Anointing that dwells in me (2 Corinthians 3:18).

O Lord, I am so hungry for You. You are so precious to me. I love You more than life itself. I desire You more than silver or gold. Fill me with Your precious Holy Spirit. Give me a deep yearning and hunger for You. Teach me Your ways, reveal Your holiness, Your majesty, and Your love to me. Unite my heart to fear and reverence you (Psalm 86:11). Fill me with Your Spirit of prayer (Zechariah 12:10), and self-control (2 Timothy 1:7). I receive Your grace and sufficiency to walk in love, faith and holiness (Hebrews 12:28). I love You, Jesus. In Your name and by the power of Your Spirit I am victorious over the enemy, the devil. I declare that no weapon formed against me, my family, my pastor, or my church shall prosper (Isaiah 54:17). Thanks be to You, Father God, Who always causes me to triumph through Christ, the Anointed and His anointing (2 Corinthians 2:14). Jesus, I have decided to come after You, deny myself, take up my cross daily and follow You (Luke 9:23). I bless You, Lord. Amen.

Today's Resolution

"This is the day the Lord has made, I will rejoice and be glad in

it" (Psalm 118:24).

I refuse to live in the regrets and resentments of yesterday. I will not curse or rehearse them. I forgive and release them, and trust God to reverse them. I will not be anxious or fearful about tomorrow (Philippians 4:6), for the Lord Himself is my Shepherd. He goes before me. I shall not want (Psalm 23:1). I put my trust in Him.

I look to Jesus today, as the Author and Finisher of my faith (Hebrews 12:2). Today, I press toward the mark for the prize of the high calling of God in Christ (Philippians 3:14). I strive to become more conformed to the image of Christ (Romans 8:29). Today, I choose to walk in the Spirit by walking in love (Galatians 5:16). I put off self-consciousness, attention-seeking, arrogance, and every prideful thought and action (Philippians 2:3). I put on humility as my clothing today (I Peter 5:5).

I choose the pathways of righteousness and truth. I will speak the truth always and trust the Lord with the results (Ephesians 4:24-25). I seek not my own will, but the will of my Lord (John 4:24). I serve Christ today by serving others (Matthew 25:40). I will hold forth the Word of Life and touch someone with the good news of Christ, my Lord and Saviour (Philippians 2:15-16). My steps are ordered by the Lord (Psalm 37:23). My timing is in God (Psalm 31:15) so I am in the right place at the right time.

I do not intend to sin today, but if I do, I will be quick to repent and ask for forgiveness, knowing that the Lord is faithful and just to forgive me my sins and to cleanse me from all unrighteousness (I John 1:9). I have no intention of stumbling today, but if I do, I will pick myself up, brush myself off, and go on by the grace of God (Proverbs 24:16).

I do not give up and I will never quit. My heart is steadfast, trusting in the Lord. I have a spirit of faith, love, power and self-control (2 Timothy 1:7). The Lord is on my side, I will not fear (Psalm 118:6).

I call myself healthy, wealthy, and wise. By Jesus' stripes I was healed (1 Peter 2:24). Divine health belongs to me. I am rich in Christ (2 Corinthians 8:9). I am a giver, and God causes all grace and favour to abound towards me (2 Corinthians 9:8). My needs are met (Philippians 4:19). Christ is my wisdom (1 Corinthians 1:30). I know what to do in every situation by the Spirit of the Lord, as I look to God and wait on Him (James 1:5). I am blessed! I call myself successful!

"They that know Your Name will put their trust in You" (Psalm 9:10).

Trust In Jehovah

God, You are my salvation. I will trust and not be afraid, because You are Jehovah my strength (Isaiah 12:2). I trust in You with all my heart, and I do not lean on my own understanding and reasoning. In all my ways I acknowledge You, and You will make my paths straight (Proverbs 3:5-6). Your love never fails. Your mercy is from everlasting to everlasting on those who fear You and who put their trust in You (Psalm 103:17).

Lord, You are a refuge in times of trouble. They that know Your name and are acquainted with Your mercy, will confidently put their trust in You (Psalm 9:9-10).

Lord, You are revealed to me as my life and all that I need in every circumstance (Exodus 6:3). You are my high tower (Proverbs 18:10), my strength, my joy, my defense, my deliverer, my protection, my healer, my peace, my salvation and my wholeness. Lord Jehovah, You are my Shepherd, I shall not want (Psalm 23:1). You are the great I AM to me (Exodus 3:14).

Lord, You are on my side, I will not fear (Psalm 118:6). My heart is fixed. I will sing and give You praise (Psalm 57:7). I am kept in Your perfect peace. My mind is stayed on You. I trust in You, Lord Jehovah (Isaiah 26:3).

I am like a tree planted by the waters, which spreads out its roots by the river. When the heat comes, I have nothing to fear. My leaves stays green. I go on bearing fruit in days of drought (Jeremiah 17:8)

The Word and I

My innermost being delights in the Word of God (Romans 7:22). It is my life (Deuteronomy 32:47). I exalt and magnify the Word above everything (Psalm 138:2). The Word of God is first place in my life (Proverbs 4:20-21). It is my top priority that the Word of God be preeminent in my life (Colossians 1:18). I am utterly ruled and governed by the Word of God.

I am a new man (2 Corinthians 5:17), over whom Satan has no dominion (Colossians 1:13). God has imparted His own nature, eternal life to me (2 Peter 1:4). The very character of God is being built into my life through the Word. The Word is a part of the Father Himself. The Word is the Father speaking to me. I feed on the Word. I breathe the Word of God into my spirit as I read and meditate in God's Word. The Word of God is the joy and the rejoicing of my heart (Jeremiah 15:16).

No Word of God is void of power (Luke 1:37). The Word of God is Spirit and Life (John 6:63), and full of power (Hebrews 4:12). Through the Word I see myself the way God sees me. There is nothing I cannot do, cannot have and cannot be, because the Word of God is working mightily in me (1 Thessalonians 2:13).

I have a right attitude towards God's Holy Word (Proverbs 13:13). My heart stands in awe of the Word (Psalm 119:161).

His Matchless Name

Hallowed be Your Name, O Lord (Matthew 7:9). You are worthy, O Lord, to receive glory, honour, power and majesty. For You have created all things, and for Your pleasure they are created (Revelation 4:11). Holy and reverend is Your name (Psalm 111:9). I give to You, Lord, the glory due to Your name, and worship You, Lord, in the beauty of Holiness (Psalm 29:2). I praise Your name, Lord, for You commanded and they were created (Psalm 148:5). You uphold all things by the Word of Your power (Hebrews 1:3). They that know Your name will put their trust in You for You, Lord, has not forsaken them that seek You (Psalm 9:10). Some trust in chariots, some trust in horses, but I remember the name of the Lord my God (Psalm 20:7). Through You Lord will I push down our enemies, through Your name will I tread them under that rise up against me (Psalm 44:5).

In God I boast all the day long and praise Your name forever. Selah! (Psalm 44:8). You have given a banner to me that it may be displayed because of the truth (Psalm 60:4). I rejoice in Your salvation and in Your name I will set up my banner (Psalm 20:5). Jehovah-Nissi is my God (Exodus 17:15), and His banner over me is love (Song of Solomon 2:4). Jehovah-Shammah is present with me. The enemy flees before me

(Ezekiel 48:35). Jehovah-Shalom reigns over me (Judges 6:24). He shall bruise the enemy under me (Romans 16:20), and make them ashes under the soles of my feet (Malachi 4:3). He sent redemption to His people (Psalm 111:9). He saved me for His name's sake that He might make His power to be known (Psalm 106:8).

Blessed be the Lord Who has not given me as a prey to their teeth. My soul is escaped as a bird out of the snare of the fowlers. The snare is broken and I escaped. My help is in the name of the Lord, who made heaven and earth (Psalm 124:6-8). I trust in the Lord and I shall be as mount Zion which cannot be moved but abide forever (Psalm 125:1). The name of the Lord is a strong tower, the righteous run into it, and I am safe (Proverbs 18:10). My heart rejoices in Him because I trust in His Holy name (Psalm 33:21). I trust in Your mercy my God forever and ever, I wait upon Your name, for it is good before Your saints (Psalm 52:8,9). Your name is faithful and true for You said in Revelation 19:11 that Your faithfulness and Your mercy shall be with him, and in Your name shall His horn be exalted (Psalm 89:24). Because I set my love upon You, therefore You will deliver me. You will set me on high because I know Your name (Psalm 91:14). Quicken me, and I will call upon Your name (Psalm 80:18). Your name is near Your wondrous works declare (Psalm 75:1).

Unite my heart to fear Your name (Psalm 86:11). In Your name shall I rejoice all the day and in Your righteousness shall I be exalted (Psalm 89:16). Let not the oppressed return ashamed; let the poor and needy praise Your name (Psalm 74:21). Your name shall endure forever, Your name shall continue as long as the sun, and men shall be blessed in You. All nations shall call You blessed (Psalm 72:17). I magnify You Lord and I exalt Your name (Psalm 34:3). For Your name alone is excellent. Your glory is above the earth and heaven (Psalm 148:13). I praise Your great and terrible name for it is Holy (Psalm 99:3). I extol You who ride upon the heavens by Your name JAH, and I rejoice before You (Psalm 68:4). I sing forth the honor of Your name and make Your praise glorious (Psalm 66:4). Blessed be Your glorious name forever (Psalm 72:19). I praise Your name for Your loving-kindness and Your truth (Psalm 138:2). According to Your name O God so is Your praise to the end of the earth (Psalm 48:10). I lift up my hands in Your name (Psalm 63:4). My Father who art in heaven hallowed be Your name, for Yours is the kingdom and the power and glory forever and ever, amen (Matthew 6:9,13).

The Name of Jesus

The name of Jesus is above all names. The name of Jesus is greater than every name. The name of Jesus has authority in Heaven, in earth and under the earth. The name of Jesus has authority at the throne of God. The name of Jesus belongs to me. In the name of Jesus I have authority over demons and sickness. Jesus has authorized me, as a child of God, to use His name. I will use His name against my enemies: hell, demons, sicknesses, diseases, sin, oppression, depression, poverty and lack. The Master said, "I shall know the truth and the truth shall make me free" and whom the Son sets free is free indeed. Now I do know the truth. Satan, you are a defeated foe. You have been dethroned. Jesus has defeated you. Demons, all evil spirits and Satan himself are subject to the name of Jesus.

All Heaven, earth and hell know that every knee must bow at the name of Jesus. For God has raised Jesus from the dead and seated Him at His own right hand far above all principalities, powers, might and dominion, and has given

Him a name supreme to every name. That name belongs to me. That name is full of power and majesty, glory and authority. Satan you were once my master and I was your slave, but now I have been delivered from your authority and established in the Kingdom of Christ. In Him I have redemption. I have power and dominion over you. I am your master because Jesus made me master over all evil power and over all demons. In the name of Jesus your power is broken over my spirit, soul and body. In the name of Jesus your power is broken over my family and over my finances. In Jesus' mighty name I take authority over any way you would try to deceive and dominate me and I bring your schemes and devices to naught. I proclaim my deliverance and victory. I am free from the devil and demons. I am free from sicknesses and diseases. I am free from pain, oppression and depression. I am free from poverty and lack. I am free from fear, anxiety and unbelief. In the name of Jesus I am free indeed.

All that Jesus has accomplished, all of His power and His authority and the might of all His conquests are invested in His name. That name belongs to me. I am thoroughly furnished with all that I need to meet the enemy in combat from day to day, and be victorious, not just once in a while but every single day of my life. I shall put the enemy to flight and enjoy victory in every fight. I am more than a conqueror through Him that loved me. I refuse to be defeated. I will stand my ground. I will stand in His name, for it is a high tower unto me. I will stand my ground and enjoy the fullness of all the blessings that belong to me. I will stand my ground and whatever I do, I will do all in the omnipotent name of Jesus and bring into reality in my life and the lives of others what Jesus has already accomplished on my behalf. I have found the truth. I have found the way.

I have found the life. I have found Jesus. I have found the key to open the boundless resources, the riches of His glory, the hidden treasures of wisdom and knowledge that are in Him. I have found the key to the unsearchable riches of Christ. Everything that is in Christ is in His name. I have the key that He has given me, and that key is His name—Jesus. He is my Lord and my Saviour. He is my High Priest and Intercessor. He is my Shepherd and my Advocate. He is the surety of a better covenant. He lives in me, and in Him I live and move and have my being. O blessed be the name of the Lord.

(I have obtained The Name of Jesus confession several years ago. I am unsure of the original source. This confession has been a blessing to me over the years and I believe it will bless you also.)

Deliverance From Pornography

Whatsoever is born of God overcomes the world, the flesh, and the devil. This is how the manifestation of the victory comes—by faith; my correct believing and speaking in accordance to the truth of God's Word (1 John 5:4; 2 Corinthians 4:13). Whom Jesus has set free, is free indeed. I am born again. I am set free by the power of God, in the name of Jesus, by virtue of the new birth (John 8:36; Galatians 5:1). The old man has been crucified and nailed to the cross with Christ, so that my body might be made ineffective and inactive for evil, and so that I may no longer be a servant of sin (Romans 6:6). I belong to Christ and I have crucified the flesh (the godless human nature) with its ungodly passions, appetites and desires (Galatians 5:14). I am dead to the world and dead to the flesh by means of the Cross of Christ. The world and the flesh are dead to me; they have no legal claim in my life.

I despise pornography and sin. It is evil and it is a weapon of the devil, designed to enslave and destroy my future and me. But in the name of Jesus I give no place to sin and pornography in my life (Ephesians 4:27). I bind you and I cast you out of my mind, my flesh and my life in the name of Jesus (Matthews 18:18). Pornography and every unclean spirit *go from me* in the name of Jesus! Pornography, I am talking to you. I am dead to you and you are dead to me (Galatians 6:14). I have overcome you by the Blood of the Lamb, and the word of my testimony. I live my life to please God, not myself (Revelation 12:11). Jesus is my Saviour and Lord. Jesus is in my life to give me His own life. His life is abundant life. I receive the abundant, pure, clean, rich and holy life of God as my very own (John 10:10). I repent of all sin, and Father, in the name Jesus, I ask you to forgive me and cleanse me from all sin and all unrighteousness. Purge me by the holy Blood of Christ. May the fire of God burn every unholy desire out of my life. I receive forgiveness and total deliverance in the name of Jesus (Isaiah 4:4). I am constantly being renewed in the spirit and attitude of my mind.

I put on the new man, which is like God, created in righteousness and true holiness (Ephesians 4:23, 27). Thank God that the Word is working mightily in me and coming to pass in my life.

Note: This confession and prayer can be adapted and used for other areas where deliverance is needed

The Anointing

Father, I choose to walk upright before You, coveting, cherishing, and watchfully guarding Your presence, Your anointing, Your glory, and Your power in my life and upon my life. Grant me wisdom and sensitivity to Your Spirit. Grant me self-control to never manipulate, misuse, or misrepresent the anointing of Your Spirit. May I never use the anointing to draw attention to myself in a self-seeking, selfish, boastful or vainglorious way. May I always be led by Your Spirit. May the anointing of Your Spirit be manifested for Your glory and for the witness and the testimony of the resurrection of my Lord and Saviour Jesus Christ. Let me be always clothed with humility, with meekness, with wisdom, and with the fear of God. Perfect me in holiness in every area of my life. I ask these things in Jesus' name, and I receive them by faith with thanksgiving and praise to Your Holy name, Jehovah M'Kaddesh. Amen.

God's Love in Me

I am born of God. I am born of love (1 John 4:7). The unconditional love of God has been poured out in my heart through the Holy Spirit (Romans 5:5). This mighty, steadfast love of God teaches me how to act and react in every situation. The love of God constrains and dominates me (2 Corinthians 5:14).

Through the love of God, I am forbearing with and forgiving to others (Colossians 3:13). I love my enemies and wish them well. I bless those that curse me. I look for opportunities to do good to them that hate me. I pray for those who despitefully use me and persecute me (Matthew 5:44). If I am insulted, I do not insult in return. If I am abused, I do not make threats and seek vengeance. I put my trust in the Lord Who judges fairly (1 Peter 2:23).

The love of God in me causes me to endure long, and to be patient and kind. I do not allow myself to be envious or boil over with jealousy. I am neither boastful or vainglorious. I am not haughty, conceited, arrogant or inflated with pride. I am not rude or unmannerly. I am not self-seeking. I do not insist on my own rights or my own way. I am not touchy, fretful or resentful. I do not keep count of the evil or wrong done to me. I do not rejoice at injustice or unrighteousness. I rejoice when right and truth prevails.

The love of God in me bears me up under anything that comes. I am always ready to believe the best of every person. My hope never fades. I endure everything without weakening. The love of God in me never fails (1 Corinthians 13:4-8).

Section II: *Confessions*

E. Talk Right

"Death and life are in the power of the tongue, and those who love it will eat its fruit" (Proverbs 18:21).

Right Talk is Heavenly

Jesus is the High Priest of my confession (Hebrews 3:1).

I am not a non-spiritual man of the flesh, in whom the carnal nature predominates, or a mere infant in Christ unable to talk (1 Corinthians 3:1). I am the righteousness of God in Christ (2 Corinthians 5:21). I am born of the Spirit (John 3:6). I am in the earth, but not of the earth (John 17:14). My citizenship is in Heaven (Philippians 3:20). I have a right to talk heavenly, according to the spiritual, which is according to the Word of God (Philippians 1:27). My conversation is to be in conformity to God's divine will and Word (Hebrews 5:13).

I call things the way God desires them to be. I call things that are not yet manifested as though they were manifested (Romans 4:17). I am made in the likeness and image of God (Colossians 3:10). I cannot be wrong when I am agreeing with and talking like God because confessing rightly is to agree with God (Romans 3:4).

God is God! He makes the rules! He has chosen the foolishness of confessing rightly to be one of the keys or principles of the Kingdom of Heaven (1 Corinthians 1:19-29; Matthew 16:19). To confess rightly is to operate in the ways of God (Isaiah 55:8-9; Psalm 25:9; Psalm 105:7).Confessing rightly reminds God of what He has said and promised, and releases the resources of Heaven and earth to fulfill His Word in my life and circumstances (Isaiah 43:26; Jeremiah 1:12).

Say out loud: *I am not ashamed to boldly confess God's Word* (Luke 9:26). *I will let God be true and every man a liar*

(Romans 3: 4). *The mouth of the righteous shall deliver them* (Proverbs 12: 6). *I am righteous in Christ. Victory and deliverance is in my mouth* (Proverbs 18: 21). *Praise the Lord!*

I Speak Life

He has made my mouth like a sharp sword; in the shadow of His hand has He hidden me. His words in my mouth are as fire and a hammer that breaks the rocks in pieces. He has anointed my lips with grace, and seasoned them with salt, so that I know how to answer every man. The Lord put forth His hand and touched my mouth, and the Lord said unto me, *"Behold I have put my words in your mouth." "My tongue is as the pen of a ready writer, writing upon the table of the hearts of men."* He has given me the tongue of the learned that I should know how to speak a word in season to him that is weary. He awakens mine ear to hear as the learned. The Lord God has opened mine ear.

The Holy Ghost shall give me utterance, teaching me what I ought to say. Whatsoever I shall hear that I shall speak. So the words I speak shall not be my own, but even as the Father says unto me by His Spirit even so shall I speak. I will yield to the spirit of prophecy which is the testimony of Jesus, converting the soul and making wise the simple. The Word of the Lord is pure, enlightening the eyes. The words coming out of a pure heart filled with the love of God, the faith of Christ, and filled with the Spirit of God are anointed. They are spirit and life, sharper than any two-edged sword, piercing even to the dividing asunder of soul and spirit, and of the joint and marrow, and is a discerner of the thoughts and intents of the heart; neither is there any creature that is not manifest in His sight, but all things are naked and opened unto the eyes of Him with whom we have to do (Isaiah 49:2; Jeremiah 5:14; Jeremiah 23:29;

Psalm 45:2; Colossians 4:6; Jeremiah 1:9; Psalm 45:1; Proverbs 3:3; Isaiah 50:4; Ephesians 6:19; Luke 12:12; Revelation 19:10; Psalm 19: 7-8; John 6:63; Hebrews 4:12)

I refuse to be snared by the words of my mouth. I refuse to speak my own words. I will not give the devil any place in my life, marriage, family or ministry by my confession. Whatever the Father gives me to say that is what I will say. I overcome the enemy by the words of my mouth—the faith-filled words of my Father. There is no more breach in the spirit because my tongue is now a wholesome tree of life connected to the tree of life. Amen. (Proverbs 6:2; Isaiah 58:13; John 14:10; Revelation 12:11; Proverbs 15:4)

"He that is slow to anger is better than the mighty; and he that ruleth his spirit than he that taketh a city" (Proverbs 16:32).

I Talk Right

I am a child of God. I have been raised up together with Christ. I sit in a heavenly place of authority in Christ (Ephesians 2:6). I live in constant awareness of my right standing with God in Christ (Hebrews 10:2). I am the righteousness of God in Christ (2 Corinthians 5:21). I have the right, privilege and responsibility to speak like God (Romans 10:6-8). The mouth of the righteous is a well of life (Proverbs 10:11). I will not allow evil and unbelief to come out of my mouth. I am quick to hear and slow to speak (James 1:19). When I speak, I choose words of life and words filled with grace (Psalm 45:2). I will remember that Jesus said, **"not what goes into the mouth defiles a man, but that which comes out of the mouth, that defiles a man"** (Matthew 15:11). Lord, I pray, set a watch before my mouth, keep the door of my lips (Psalm 141:3) that I sin not with my tongue (Psalm 39:1). Jesus is the High Priest of my confession (Hebrews 3:1).

God's Word in My Mouth

My mouth is like a sharp sword in the hand of God (Isaiah 49:2). God's Word in my mouth is like a fire and a hammer that breaks the rocks in pieces (Jeremiah 23:29). My lips are anointed with grace and seasoned with the salt of God's Word, so that I know how to answer every man in every situation (Colossians 4:6). Christ is made unto me wisdom (1 Corinthians 1:30). The Lord has touched my mouth and put His Words in my mouth (Jeremiah 1:9). My tongue is as a pen of a ready writer (Psalm 45:1). The Lord has given me the tongue of the learned so that I should know how to speak a word in season. He awakens me morning by morning. He awakens my ear to hear as the learned (Isaiah 50:4). The Holy Spirit gives me utterance and teaches me what I am to say (Luke 12:12). Unbelief is an abomination to my lips (Proverbs 8:7). I will not be snared by the words of my mouth (Proverbs 6:2). I speak words of life and victory (Proverbs 18:21).

Section II: *Confessions*

F. Redemptive Rights

"Blessed be the God and Father of our Lord Jesus Christ, who has blessed us with every spiritual blessing in the heavenly places in Christ...In Him we have redemption through His blood, the forgiveness of sins, according to the riches of His grace" (Ephesians 1:3, 7).

1. Healing:
Healing is Mine

"Pleasant words are as a honeycomb sweet to the soul and healing to the body" (Proverbs 16:24).

The fact is Jesus has borne my grief (sicknesses, weaknesses, and distresses) and carried my sorrows and pains. He was wounded for my transgressions, He was bruised for my iniquities, and the chastisement of my peace was upon Him, and with His stripes I am healed (Isaiah 53:4,5).

As Moses lifted up the serpent in the wilderness, even so Jesus was lifted on the cross (John 3:14). Jesus became a curse for me, because it is written, "Cursed is everyone who hangs on a tree." I am redeemed from the curse of sickness and diseases (Galatians 3:13). The law of the Spirit of Life in Christ Jesus has made me free from the law of sickness and disease (Romans 8:2). The law of the Spirit of life operates in and dominates my body and life.

The law of the Spirit of Life operates by the law of faith. Faith must have a voice (Romans 4:17; 10:6-8). I give voice to my faith. Life and death is in the power of my tongue (Proverbs 18:21). I choose to speak life. The tongue of the wise promotes health (Proverbs 12:18). I say with my mouth and believe in my heart that I am the healed of the Lord. According to 1 Peter 2:24, I was healed. And if I was healed then, I am healed. I believe Isaiah's report. The merciful healing arm of the Lord is revealed to me (Isaiah 53:1). The same spirit that raised up Christ from the dead dwells in me and makes alive my body (Romans 8:11).

Sickness, you are not allowed to trespass in my body. I am the righteousness of God in Christ (2 Corinthians 5:21). I am the temple of God. I glorify God in my body and in my spirit, which belong to God (1 Corinthians 6:19,20). I say sickness nor sin is allowed in my life. Jesus is my healer. I know the truth and the truth sets me free (John 8:32). Healing is the children's bread. I have a blood bought right to healing. Healing belongs to me. Sickness, I command you in Jesus' Name, go away from me! Get out of my body and my home! I take authority over you (Luke 10:19).

God has sent His Word and healed me (Psalm 107:20). I am not ashamed, for I know whom I have believed and I am persuaded that Jesus is my Healer (2 Timothy 1:12). I bless You Lord. You forgive all my iniquities and You heal all my diseases (Psalm 103:2,3). Because I have set my love upon You, O Lord, therefore will You deliver me and set me on high, because I know Your Name is Healer. I call upon You and You will answer me. You will be with me in trouble. You will deliver me and honour me. With long life You will satisfy me and show me Your salvation (Ps. 91:14-16).

"Bless the lord O my soul and all that is within me bless His Holy Name."

Healing Confession

Name the specific sickness on the blank provided: _____ , in the Name of Jesus I bind you. Come out of my body in the Name of Jesus. Devil, you cannot kill me. By Jesus' stripes I am healed. Glory to God my Father. Thank you Lord for Your divine healing power flowing through my body. Thank You Lord for Your divine healing power making me totally whole. I shall live and testify of the healing power of God and the goodness of the Lord. Thank You Lord that by Your stripes I am healed. Jesus, You are my divine healer and You are manifesting Your healing in my _____ (name area of the body) right now.

Confess the above all the time. Confess it with boldness, authority, and faith in the Almighty God, your Father; until healing is fully manifested.

I Am Healed

"Forever, O Lord, Your word is settled in heaven" (Psalm 119: 89). Your Word says that my stomach shall be satisfied from the fruit of my mouth; from the produce of my lips I shall be filled. Your Word also says that death and life are in the power of (my) tongue. I choose life (Proverbs 18:20,21; Deuteronomy 30:19) therefore, I propose Lord that my mouth shall not transgress against You. But, by the word of my lips, I will keep away from the paths of the destroyer. Set a guard Lord over my mouth; keep watch over the door of my lips lest I sin with my tongue. I will keep my mouth with a bridle (Psalm 141:3, 39;1). I will hold fast to the confession of my faith without wavering for you are faithful that promised, and will watch over your word to perform it (Hebrews 10:23; Jeremiah 1:12).

Jesus, my Lord, You Yourself took my infirmity and bore my sickness (Matthew 8:17). You bore my sins in Your own body on the tree, and by Your stripes I am healed (1 Peter 2:24; Isaiah 53: 4,5). Jesus, You always live to make intercession for me, that I may walk in divine health and be the righteousness of God in you - for as You are, so am I in this world (Hebrews 7:25; 2 Corinthians 5:21; 1 John 4:17). In you I live and move and have my being (Acts 17:28). I am in Christ Jesus, and I do not walk according to the flesh, but according to the spirit.

The law of the spirit of life in Christ Jesus has made me free from the law of sin, death, sickness, disease, and pain (Romans 8:2). I abide in your Word, Lord Jesus. I am your disciple indeed. I know the truth and the truth made me free. I am free indeed from the law of sin and death, and I walk and live in divine health (John 8:32:36). The Spirit of God Who raised Jesus from the dead dwells in me, God Who raised Christ from the dead gives life to my mortal body through His Spirit Who dwells in me (Romans 8:11). I shall not die, but live, and declare the works of the Lord and will praise Him (Psalm 118:17,19). Thank you Lord Jesus, You are the Lord that heals me from all diseases. You sent Your Word, and healed me (Psalm 107:20; 103:3). Your Word in me is alive and powerful, piercing even to the joints and marrow. Your Word is health to all my flesh, and my bones (Proverbs 4:21 16:24).

I shall not be satisfied until I awake in your likeness (Psalm 17:15). I hereby do declare with my mouth and believe in my heart that by Jesus' stripes I am healed (Romans 10:10; 1 Peter 2:24; Isaiah 53:5).

I challenge you to spend one hour a day in the pages of this book and see the harvest of righteousness that will spring up in your life (2 Corinthians 9:10).

2. Protection: Divine Protection

The Lord is my protection. The Lord God is my strength and shield (Psalm 27:1). He will give grace and glory (Psalm 84:11); The Lord is a wall of fire around about me (Zechariah 2:5). The Lord covers me with His feathers. There shall no evil befall me, neither shall any plague come near me. My Father God shall give His angels charge over me to keep me in all my ways to protect me. They shall bear me up in their hands lest I dash my foot against a stone (Psalm 91:4; 10-12).

The angels of the Lord encamps around about me (Psalm 34:7). I do fear the Lord and I put my trust in Him. He is my help and my shield (Psalm 115:11). The Lord is my healer and keeps me well and healthy (Exodus 15:26). I declare these things in the authority of the name of Jesus Christ my Lord (John 14:14).

3. Prosperity: My Needs are Met

My belief is based on the Word of God and the faithfulness of my heavenly Father, and the Blood sworn promises He has given me. I am not moved by what I see. I do not believe according to reasoning. My belief is not based on the channels of supply that I can reason. I believe according to God. My needs are met according to His riches. My needs are supplied through His channels, in glory by Christ Jesus and His anointing. My faith in God, Jesus, and the Word is the substance of things I hope for and the evidence I have for the things not seen. Through the abundance of grace and the gift of righteousness, I do reign in this life by Christ Jesus, my Shepherd and Lord. I shall not want.

(Luke 1:38; 2 Corinthians 4:18; Proverbs 3:5; Philippians 4:19; Hebrews 11:1; Romans 5:17; Psalm 23:1).

Financial Deliverance

Christ, the Anointed One and His anointing in me, is my hope of glory. Christ is my expectation of financial deliverance, and financial increase (Colossians 1:27). The supply of the Spirit of Christ (Philippians 1:19) destroys the yokes of poverty and removes the burdens of lack in my life (Isaiah 10:27).

Christ has redeemed me from the curse of the law. I am redeemed from the curse of sin, poverty, and death (Galatians 3:13). I seek first the Kingdom of God and His righteousness, and all my needs are being met (Matthew 6:33; Philippians 4:19). I give to the cause of Christ, and help meet the needs of others. Men are giving into my bosom, good measure, pressed down, shaken together, and running over (Luke 6:38). God is causing all grace and favour to abound towards me (2 Corinthians 9:8). The blessings of Abraham are overtaking me (Galatians 3:14). The anointing of prosperity is operating in my life (Deuteronomy 8:18). The anointing of El-Shaddai is operating in my life, so that all my needs are met, my bills are paid, my debts are cancelled, and I have more than enough to abound and to give to every good work (2 Corinthians 9:8). I am not anxious for anything. My heavenly Father cares for me and He knows what I have need of, even before I ask (Matthew 6:31-32). The Lord, El-Shaddai, Jehovah-Jireh is my source and supply. I put my trust in Him.

I magnify the Lord and shout for joy. I favour and support the cause of Christ. I am on the Lord's side, and the Lord is on my side. He takes pleasure in my prosperity (Psalm 35:27). I am a tither and a giver (Deuteronomy 26), and God rebukes the devourer for my sake (Malachi 3:11).

Satan, I bind you in the name of Jesus, and forbid you from operating in the financial affairs of my life, my family, and my church. I command you to take your hands off of my finances. I declare that money comes to me now! Angels of the living God I release you to bring finances and prosperity to me (Hebrews 1:14) in the name of Jesus.

Financial Prosperity

The supply of the Spirit of Christ through the anointing of God in us destroys the yokes of poverty and removes the burdens of lack. The anointing of El-Shaddai operates in my life, so that I have more than enough to meet every need and pay every bill and remove every debt. All my needs are met according to His riches in glory by Christ Jesus. I have more than enough so that I can meet the needs of others. I am more than a conqueror over bills and debts through the anointing. I am anxious for nothing. My Heavenly Father cares for me and knows what I have need of, and He is my source and supply. I seek first His Kingdom and His Righteousness, and all things are added unto me. Christ by His anointing has redeemed me from the curse of the law, being made a curse for me.

Now the blessings of Abraham are overtaking me. Men are giving into my bosom: good measure, pressed down, shaken together, and running over. God is making all grace to abound toward me, so that I, having all sufficiency in all things, am able to abound to every good work. I magnify the Lord and shout for joy, because He desires for me to prosper and be in health, even as my soul prospers. My God takes pleasure in my prosperity. I bind you devil and kick you out of all the financial affairs and circumstances of my life in Jesus' name. I release God's angels now to bring finances and prosperity to me. I call all my bills paid. I declare all my debts cancelled. I have much money left over to give to others. I am blessed and I am a blessing to others. Thank you, Lord, for sending prosperity today. Amen!

(Philippians 1:19; 2 Corinthians 1:21; Isaiah 10:27; Genesis 17:1-2; Philippians 4:19; Romans 8:37; Philippians 4:6; 1 Peter 5:7; Matthew 6:32-33; Galatians 3:13-14; Deuteronomy 28:2; Luke 6:38; 2 Corinthians 9:8; Psalm 35:27; 3 John 2; Matthew 18:18-19; Psalm 118:25).

Remaining Steadfast in Prosperity

I will not allow pressure or circumstances to change my confession. My confession is based entirely on God's Word. My confession is based entirely on His faithfulness, and His promises to me. My faith has a voice, a voice of victory. I live in a realm where nothing is impossible to me, because I am hooked up with the God Who is omnipotent, omniscient, and omnipresent.

God meets my every need, and I have an abundant supply. I will never be broke another day in my life. I plead the blood of Jesus Christ over my finances. God is my father and He has provided for me to be prosperous.

Debt, get away from me! Distresses, go from me! Discontentment, leave me, in Jesus' Name! Satan take your hands off my finances! I will not believe your lies anymore. God does not want me, His child, to live in poverty. Poverty is a lie from you, Satan, and it is also a lie from religion and tradition. God wants me prosperous, and I am in agreement with God from this time forward. I resist the thoughts of poverty, doubt, and failure. I call myself prosperous and successful in Jesus' Name. Thank you Lord, Hallelujah!

I am a believer. I am a giver. And I am anointed to prosper. Lack, go from me in Jesus' name. It is good to be part of the family of God. It is good to belong to God. The Lord is my

Shepherd, I shall not want (Psalm 23:1).

Established in Prosperity

Christ has redeemed me from the curse of the law. Christ has redeemed me from poverty; Christ has redeemed me from sickness; Christ has redeemed me from spiritual death (Galatians 3:13-14; Deuteronomy 28). Jesus has delivered me from poverty and given me wealth. He set me free from sickness and has given me health. He has delivered me from spiritual death and has given me eternal life (2 Corinthians 8:9; Isaiah 53:5-6; John 10:10, 5:24).

God is able to make all grace (every favour and earthly blessing) come to me in abundance, so that I may always and under all circumstances be self-sufficient, possessing enough to require no aid or support and furnished in abundance for every good work and charitable donation.

Thus I will be enriched in all things and in every way, so that I can be generous. I delight myself in the Lord and He gives me the desires of my heart (Psalm 37:4). I have given and it is given to me good measure, pressed down, shaken together, running over. People give to me all the time (Luke 6:38). With the measure I mete, it is measured to me. I sow bountifully therefore I reap bountifully. I give cheerfully, and my God has made all grace abound toward me. Having all sufficiency of all things, I do abound to all good works (2 Corinthians 9:6-8). I do not lack any good thing, for my God supplies all of my need according to His riches in glory by Christ Jesus (Philippians 4:19).

The Lord is my shepherd and I do not want because Jesus was made poor so I through His poverty might have abundance. Jesus came that I might have life and have it more abundantly (Psalm 23:1; 2 Corinthians 8:9; John 10:10). I have received the gift of righteousness, therefore, I do reign as a king in life by Jesus Christ (Romans 5:17). The Lord has pleasure in the prosperity of His servant, and Abraham's blessings are mine (Psalm 35:27; Galatians 3:14). I seek first the kingdom of God and His righteousness, so all things I need are added unto me (Matthew 6:33). God, Who did not withhold or spare even His own Son, but gave Him up for us all, freely gives me all things (Romans 8:32).

The powerful, active, living Word of God is always on my lips. I meditate on it day and night that I may observe and do what is written in it. As a result, I'm prosperous and successful. And since I'm willing and obedient, I eat the good of the land (Hebrews 4:12; Joshua 1:8; Isaiah 1:19). The Lord teaches me to profit and leads me by the way I should go. Blessings are coming upon me and overtaking me, as the Lord daily loads me with benefits (Isaiah 48:17; Deuteronomy 28:2; Psalm 68:19). I have faith and I do not doubt. Whatever I ask for in prayer believing, I will receive it from the Lord, Who is able to do exceeding abundantly above all that I ask or think (Matthew 21:21-22; Ephesians 3:20). I ask and it is given to me; I seek and find; I knock and the door is opened for me (Matthew 7:7-11).

I am the righteousness of God in Christ Jesus. Therefore the wealth of the sinner, which is laid up for me, is finding its way into my hands. God is giving sinners the task of gathering and storing up wealth to hand it over to me (2 Corinthians 5:21; Proverbs 13:22; Ecclesiastes 2:26). The Lord goes before me, levels the mountains, and makes the crooked places straight. He gives me the treasures of darkness and hidden riches of secret places (Isaiah 45:2-3). God gives me seed because I'm a sower. He will multiply the seed I have sown (1 Corinthians 9:8-11). I prosper in every way and my body keeps well (3 John 2).

Restoration

Satan, I bind you in the name of Jesus. I command you to loose my finances, and release the supplies in the earth I need. I forbid you Satan and all your demons, from operating in the financial affairs of my life, my family, or my ministry. Jesus is my Lord and my Shepherd, I shall not want. Furthermore, I command you devil to restore seven fold all you have stolen from me and my family. I receive complete restoration in every area of my life. My finances, my soul, my relationship in God, and much more are totally restored. My stolen years are restored. My youth is renewed as an eagle. My wallet, cupboards, bank accounts, and my storehouses are full of finances, goods, wheat, and much more. My vats and life are overflowing with wine and oil. The time of restoration of all good things in my life is here.

(Matthew 16:19; Proverbs 6:31; Psalm 103:5; Proverbs 3:10; Isaiah 42:22).

Tithing Confession
(Based on Deuteronomy 26)

Father, in Jesus' name I thank you that I am the redeemed of the Lord. I was once lost and without you, and on the way to hell. However, I called on the name of Jesus, and You saved me. You delivered me from the devil's kingdom. I am now Your very own child, and you are my very own Father. Thank You for Your salvation. I rejoice in every good thing You are doing in my life and in my church. I praise and bless you. Jesus You are my Lord and High Priest. I bring my tithes and my offering to You in obedience to Your Word and Your voice. I worship You with it.

Now, Lord, look down from Your holy habitation, and bless me as You said. Send now prosperity and increase. Let Your covenant of increase be established with me. As a tither, I declare in Jesus' name, the devourer is rebuked for my sake. Poverty and lack I am talking to you. Go away from me. I am free from you. Grace and favour, come abound towards me. Goodness and mercy come follow me. My needs are met! The needs of my church are met. Money comes to me now! Promotion comes to me now! Employment comes to me now! Increase comes to me now. I praise You Lord.

Money Comes to Me Because:

1. Money comes to me now because God my Father is possessor of the heavens and the earth and He wills that I prosper (3 John 2; Genesis 14:22).

2. Money comes to me now because I am a child of God and it is my Father's good pleasure to give me the kingdom (Luke 12:32).

3. Money comes to me now because it belongs to me. All things are mine (1 Corinthians 3:21).

4. Money comes to me now because when God gave me His Son, Jesus, He also freely gave me all things (Romans 8:32).

5. Money comes to me now because I am an heir of God and a joint heir with Christ of all things (Romans 8:17; Hebrews 1:2).

6. Money comes to me now because I am wealthy on the inside. The kingdom of God is within me (Luke 17:21).

7. Money comes to me now because I am a money magnet. I do not pursue money but money is attracted to me.

8. Money comes to me now because I seek first the kingdom of God and His righteousness. And all things including money is added to me (Matthew 6:33).

9. Money comes to me now because I am a giver and it is given back to me good measure, pressed down, shaken together, and running over, men give into my bosom (Luke 6:38).

10. Money comes to me now because I am redeemed from poverty and lack (2 Corinthians 8:9; Galatians 3:13).

11. Money comes to me now because I have a blood covenant and the Lord is my shield and my exceeding great reward (Genesis 15:1)

12. Money comes to me now because I am loaded. The Lord, El-Shaddai, daily loads me with benefits (Psalm 68:19).

13. Money comes to me now because I have received power to get wealth so that God's covenant of prosperity might be established in my life, and that I might be a distribution center for God, so that His covenant may be established in the earth (Deuteronomy 8:18).

14. Money comes to me now because I am willing and

obedient. Therefore, I shall eat the good of the land (Isaiah 1:19).

15. Money comes to me now because I favor God's righteous cause and the Lord takes delight in my prosperity (Psalm 35:27).

16. Money comes to me now because angels who are ministering spirits are at work on my behalf channeling money to me (Hebrews 1:14).

17. Money comes to me now because God has commanded the blessing on my storehouse and everything I set my hand to (Deuteronomy 28:8).

18. Money comes to me now because I delight in God's Word and I fear and reverence the Lord. Wealth and riches shall be in my house (Psalm 112:1-2).

19. Money comes to me now because the Holy Spirit teaches me how to profit (Isaiah 48:17).

20. Money comes to me now because the Lord is my shepherd, I shall not want (Psalm 23:1).

21. Money comes to me now because I am living in the last days when the wealth that the sinner has laid up is being transferred to the righteous, that means me (Proverbs 13:22).

Let these Word-Seeds be as a frontlet before your eyes and say them constantly that they may get into your heart.

Eight Financial Nuggets

WHEN YOU GIVE:

- Never let your seed travel alone.
- Always release your faith when you give.

HOW?

When you give...

1. Believe that you will receive your harvest. Say, "I receive my harvest". Be specific (Mark 11:24).

2. Don't drop your seed in the bucket without claiming God's promises. It is like putting seed on top of the ground where the birds can steal it (Matthew 13:4).

3. Dig a hole and plant your seed by claiming specific promises as you give (Matthew 13:8).

4. Resist fear. Give with joy and expectation. Remember giving is not loss but gain (Matthew 19:22). It shall be given back to you good measure, pressed down, shaken together, and running over shall men give into your bosom (Luke 6:38).

5. Mix your giving with thanksgiving (Psalm 50:14). Say out loud, "Thank You Lord for the privilege of giving to You. Thank You Lord for multiplying my seed sown and giving me a harvest" (2 Corinthians 9:10).

6. Remind yourself by reminding God that you have an active covenant with Him that covers every area of your life (Deuteronomy 26:1-19; Malachi 3:6-12; Hebrews 7:8).

7. Take time to ask and listen to God as to what to give. Because God will not ask you to give what you don't have. God gives seed to the sower (2 Corinthians 9:10). There is always a blessing with obeying God's voice (Deuteronomy. 28:1,2).

8. Do not grow weary and faint in doing right, for in due season you shall reap if you do not relax your courage and faint (Galatians 6:9).

Remember, faith and obedience always please God.

Sowing and God's Prosperity System

It is the Father's will, joy, delight, and good pleasure to see His children prosper (Ps. 35: 27; Luke 12: 32; 3 John 2). Our Father God has made several provisions for us to prosper, increase, and be successful.

- He has given us precious promises (2 Peter 1:4), and His faithful Word (Deuteronomy 11: 18-21; Psalm 1:1-3).

- He has redeemed us from the curse, which includes poverty and lack (Galatians 3: 13-14; 2 Corinthians 8: 9; Psalm 23: 1).

- He has given us a covenant of prosperity (Genesis 17: 2; Genesis 22: 17-18; Galatians 3: 7,29).

- He has given us a system of prosperity, called seedtime and harvest (Genesis 8: 22) or sowing and reaping (Galatians 6: 6-10). It is a system that includes tithing and giving (Deuteronomy 26:12; Malachi 3:10; Hebrews 7:8; 1 Corinthians 16:2).

* He has anointed and empowered us to prosper (Deuteronomy 8:18).

* He has sent the Holy Spirit to teach us to profit (Isaiah 48:17), and to lead and guide us (Psalm 32:8; John 16:13).

* He has even assigned angels to help us (Hebrews 1:14; Psalm 103:20; Genesis 24:40).

Here are requirements to operate in God's prosperity system:

* Knowledge. We must study God's Word on prosperity, so we can think right (3 John 2; Proverbs 23: 7; Hosea 4: 6).

* We must believe God's Word and have faith (Romans 4: 16; Hebrews 11: 6).

* We must walk in obedience to the Word, and the Holy Spirit's leading (Isaiah 1: 19, Job 36:11).

* It is important to tithe and give (Matthew 23:23; Luke 6:38; Proverbs 11: 25; Proverbs 3:9,10).

See Tithing articles in Section I.

4. My Children:
My Children- Part 1

Father, in the name of Jesus, I pray and confess that Your Word prevails over my children (Acts 19:20). I surround them with love and faith. My children are disciples of Christ, taught of the Lord, and obedient to Your will (Isaiah 54:13). Give my children a heart to seek after You and to fear You, and know You intimately. Your angels have charge over my children to accompany, defend, and preserve them in all their ways (Ps. 91:11). Lord You are their refuge and fortress (Psalm 91:2) and the glory and the lifter of their heads (Psalm 3:3).My children are the head and not the tail, and shall be above only and not beneath (Deu. 28: 13). I receive your grace Lord to raise up my children in the discipline, counsel, and admonition of the Lord (Ephesians 6:1-3). Heavenly Father, I thank you for perfecting that which concerns me (Ps. 138:8). I commit and cast the care of my children once and for all on to You (1 Pet. 5:7). I commit them into Your able hands (2 Timothy 1:12).

My Children- Part 2

Father God, Your Word promises that You will show mercy to your anointed and to his seed forever. I ask and believe You for mercy to all my children. I claim Your Word that declares: believe on the Lord Jesus Christ and you shall be saved and your household. I plead the Blood of the Lamb of God for my household. I sprinkle the speaking blood of the Lord Jesus on each of their lives. I cover them with the precious, sanctifying, cleansing, and protecting Blood of Christ, the Lamb. Lord, teach them Your ways and cause them to walk in truth. Unite their heart to fear Your Name. I declare the hand of the Lord is upon them and with them.

I believe your Word, Father, that you will contend with him that contends with my children. You will save my children and establish them in righteousness. They shall be taught of You and great shall be their peace. Reveal Your glory and lordship to them, and let Your beauty be upon them. I declare Your covenant blessing upon their lives, and they shall be mighty upon the earth. They will possess the gates of their enemies. My children are my heritage from the Lord. They are for signs and for wonders in the earth. God's perfect plan for their lives shall be accomplished.

Father, I thank you for circumcising their hearts to love you with all their hearts and all their soul, and for making you their Lord and God. Rejoice over them, O Lord, for good. Give them a heart to seek after You and to know You. Let their hope be in You and forget not Your works, but that they keep your commandments. I thank you for Your salvation, protection, mercy, love, and for Your bountiful provision in their lives. In Jesus' name, pour out Your Spirit upon my children.

I declare in Jesus' name that my children are free from the power of the devil. In Jesus' name they shall not walk according to the prince of the power of the air. In Jesus' name, I declare them free from the spirit that is now working in the sons of disobedience. They are free from walking according to the lusts of their flesh, from indulging in the desires of the flesh and of the mind. They are free from being by nature the children of wrath. God, You are rich in mercy to my children because of Your great love with which You love them. By the eye of faith, I see they are alive together with Christ and are made to sit together in heavenly places in Christ Jesus, that in the ages to come You might show the surpassing riches of Your grace in Your kindness toward them in Christ Jesus.

Father, strengthen my children with might by your Spirit in their spirit, soul, and body. I declare that Christ dwells in their hearts by faith, and they are rooted and grounded in the love of Christ, and they comprehend with all the saints the length, depth, height, and width of Your love. They also comprehend the mystery of the fellowship of Christ and know the love of Christ that passes mere knowledge, and are filled with all the fullness of God. By grace they are being saved through faith through the redemption that is in Christ Jesus not of themselves, it is a gift of God. They will walk as children of light having been delivered and set free from the kingdom of darkness and are translated into the kingdom of Christ. In Jesus' mighty name, and by His blood, I declare my children are free from the devil's dominion and influence. Every plot and scheme of the devil is brought to naught in Jesus' name. Father, I thank you because you are faithful, merciful, gracious, and will do beyond what I could ask or think according to the power of the Holy Ghost and Your mercy.

I declare the name of Jehovah over each of my children. The kingdom of God comes upon them. The will of God be fulfilled in their lives as it is in Heaven. I give you praise for Your goodness and deliverance in their lives. I thank You for giving them wisdom, favour, grace, and the fear of the Lord. You are their sufficiency. I declare that all that see them shall acknowledge them that they are the seed whom the Lord has blessed, in the name of Jesus.

I thank You for Your divine protection on them. I claim Psalm ninety-one on their behalf in the name of Jesus. I thank you for saving them. I call my children saved and filled with the Spirit of God, the Word of God, and the power of God in Jesus' name. Amen.

Dear reader for further study, please read the following passages of scripture: Psalm 147:13; Proverbs 111:21; Psalm 102:28; Isaiah 65:23; Isaiah 59:21; Jeremiah 31:17; Psalm 89:28,29; Acts 16:31; Exodus 12:13; Psalm 25:12; Isaiah 49:25; Isaiah 54:13,14; Psalm 112:2; Psalm 127:3; Jeremiah 29:11; Psalm 138:8; Ephesians 2:2-7; Ephesians 3:16-19; Ephesians 2:8; Ephesians 5:8; Colossians 1:13; Isaiah 54:17; Ephesians 3:20; Matthew 6:10; 2 Corinthians

3:5; Isaiah 61:9)

I Believe for Me and My House

Jesus is the Son of God and I yield my life to Him as my resurrected Lord. I have been translated out of the devil's kingdom of darkness, and I am now in the Kingdom of Christ, the Kingdom of Light (Colossians 1:13). I have eternal life dwelling in me (John 5:24).

In the name of Jesus, I cast out devils. In the name of Jesus, I lay hands on the sick and they recover (Mark 16:17-18). God confirms His Word with signs following as I preach and share about Jesus with others (Mark 16:20). The works that Jesus did I do also and greater works (John 14:12). I can do all things through Christ who strengthens me (Phil. 4:13).

I am who God says I am. I can do what God says I can do. I have what God says I have, and I am called to what God says I am called to. I have the mind of Christ (1 Cor. 2:16). Nothing is impossible to me as a believer (Mark 9:23).

I have authority over all the works of the enemy (Luke 10:19). What I bind on earth is bound in Heaven. In the name of Jesus, I have the keys of the Kingdom of Heaven (Matt. 16:19). In the name of Jesus, I break the power of every spirit that would blind my family members from the truth of the Gospel (2 Cor. 4:4). I demolish every stronghold of reason, philosophy, tradition, religion, and any other system of thinking that would exalt itself above the truth of Christ (2 Cor. 10:4-5). I smash them with the hammer of God's Word (Jer. 23:29). I plead the Blood of Jesus and command them to be free from the enemy's grip (Zech.

9:11). According to God's Word, I believe on Jesus and every member of my family and house shall be saved (Acts 16:31). Thank You Lord for their salvation.

I belong to Jesus. I am His sheep, and I hear His voice. The voice of a stranger I will not follow (John 10:27,5). Open my ears, O Lord, to hear as the learned (Is. 50:4).

I am a giver. I give in faith, love, and mercy (Matt. 23:23). God has commanded my harvest on every seed that I sow into His Kingdom. I receive my harvest in Jesus' name. It is given back to me good measure, pressed down, shaken together, and running over. Men are giving into my bosom (Luke 6:38). I have more than enough to abound to every good work (2 Cor. 9:8).

I am blessed going in, and I am blessed going out (Deut.28:6). Goodness and mercy follow me all the days of my life (Ps.23:6). Everyone that is of the truth hears His voice (John 18:37).

Section II: *Confessions*

G. From the Psalms

"He has put a new song in my mouth. Praise to our God; Many will see it and fear, And will trust in the LORD" (Psalm 40:3)

1. Prayers, Confessions, Meditation: Victory, and Comfort from the Psalms

He shall set me up upon a Rock (Psalm 27:5). He makes my feet like hinds feet and set me upon my high places (Psalm 18:33). He teaches my hands to war, so that a bow of steel is broken by mine arms (Psalm 18:34). You have enlarged my steps under me, that my feet did not slip (Psalm 18:36). I have set the Lord always before me; because He is at my right hand, I shall not be moved (Psalm 16:8). Mine eyes are ever towards the Lord, for He shall pluck my feet out of the net (Psalm 25:15). Great deliverances gives He to His king; and show mercy to His anointed and to His seed forevermore (Psalm 18:50).

My head shall be lifted up above mine enemies round about me. Therefore will I offer in Your tabernacle sacrifices of joy. I will sing, yes, I will sing praises unto the Lord (Psalm 27:6). The Lord is my strength and He is the saving strength of His anointed (Psalm 28:8). The Lord gives strength unto me, the Lord will bless me with peace (Psalm 29:11). For Your anger endures but a moment. In Your favour is life. Weeping may endure for a night, but joy comes in the morning (Psalm 30:5). You have turned for me my mourning into dancing. You have put off my sack cloth and girded me with gladness (Psalm 30:11). You will show me the path of life. In Your presence is fullness of joy. At Your right hand there are pleasures forevermore (Psalm 16:11). For My heart shall rejoice in You because I have trusted in Your Holy Name (Psalm 33:21). How excellent is Your loving kindness, O God, therefore the children of men put their trust under the shadow of Your wings (Psalm 36:7), My soul shall make her boast in the Lord (Psalm 34:2). I sought the Lord, and He heard me and delivered me from all my fears (Psalm 34:4). The Lord is near unto them that are of a broken heart, and saves such as be of a contrite spirit (Psalm 34:18). The Lord redeems the soul of His servants and none of them that trust in Him shall be desolate (Psalm 34:22). Make Your face to shine upon Your servant (Psalm 31:16). Let the Lord be magnified which has pleasure in the prosperity of His servant (Psalm 35:27). The salvation of the righteous is of the Lord; He is their strength in the time of trouble. And the Lord shall help them and deliver them; He shall deliver them from the wicked, and save them, because they trust in Him (Psalm 37:39-40). He has put a new song in my mouth, even praise unto our God (Psalm 40:3).

Praise from the Psalms

Reasons for Praise

It is a good thing to give thanks to You Lord, and to sing praises to Your name, O Most High (Psa1m.92:1). Praise You O Lord: for it is good to sing praise to God, for it is pleasant, and praise is comely (Psalm 147:1). For who is in the heaven that can be compared to You? Who among the sons of the mighty can be likened to You Lord? God, You are greatly to be feared in the assembly of the saints and to be held in reverence of all them that are about You (Psalm 89:6,7). Give to the Lord, O you mighty, give to the Lord glory and strength. I give to the Lord the glory due to His name, and worship the Lord in the beauty of holiness (Psalm 29:1,2). You are Holy, O You that inhabits the praises of Israel (Psalm 22:3).

You have ordained strength because of Your enemies, that You might still the enemy and the avenger (Psalm 8:2). Let the high praises of God be in my mouth, and a two edged sword in my hand, to execute vengeance upon the heathen, and punishment upon the people. To bind their kings with chains, and their nobles with fetters of iron. To execute upon them the judgement written, this honour have all His saints. I praise You O Lord (Psalm 149:6-9). You are worthy to be praised, so shall I be saved from my enemies (Psalm 18:3). Let such that love Your salvation say continually let God be magnified (Psalm 70:4).

Praise Him For

Rejoice in the Lord, you righteous and give thanks at the remembrance of His holiness (Psalm 97:12). Seven times a day do I praise You because of Your righteous Judgments (Psalm 119:164). I praise You Lord according to Your righteousness, and sing praise to the name of the Lord Most High (Psalm 7:17). Be exalted, Lord in Your own strength, so will I sing and praise Your power (Psalm 21:13). Because Your loving kindness is better than life, my lips praise You, thus I bless You while I live (Psalm 63:3,4). Oh that men would praise the Lord for His goodness and for His wonderful works to the children of men (Psalm 107:8). I sing of the mercies of the Lord forever, with my mouth I make known Your faithfulness to all generations (Psalm 89:1). I show forth Your loving kindness in the morning, and Your faithfulness every night (Psalm 92:2). According to Your name, O God, so is Your praise to the ends of the earth (Psalm 48:10).

Let them praise Your great and terrible name, for it is Holy (Psalm 99:3). I praise the name of God with a song, and magnify Him with thanksgiving (Psalm 69:30). Sing to God, sing praises to His name, extol Him who rides upon the heavens by His name Jah, and rejoice before Him (Psalm

68:4). Blessed be His glorious name forever, and let the whole earth be filled with His glory. Amen and Amen (Psalm 72:19).

Attitude in Praise

I praise You, O Lord, with my whole heart, I show forth all Your marvelous works. I am glad and rejoice in You, I sing praises to Your name, O Most High (Psalm 9:12). I praise You with my whole heart before the gods I sing praise to You. I worship toward Your Holy temple and praise Your name for Your loving kindness and for Your truth, for You have magnified Your word above all Your name (Psalm 138:1,2). Teach me Your way, O Lord, I will walk in Your truth. Unite my heart to fear Your name. I will praise You, O Lord my God, with my whole heart and I will glorify Your name forevermore (Psalm 86:11,12). Worship the Lord in the beauty of Holiness (Psalm 96:9).

How to Praise

I sing praises to God, I sing praises, I sing praises to my King, I sing praises. For God is King of all the earth, I sing praises with understanding (Psalm 47:6, 7). Lord, You are God, it is You that has made us and not we ourselves, we are Your people and the sheep of Your pasture. I enter into Your gates with thanksgiving, and into Your courts with praise, I am thankful to You, and bless Your name. ***I make a joyful noise to the Lord*** (Psalm 100:3,4). I will make Your praise glorious. O God, how terrible are You in Your works. Through the greatness of Your power shall Your enemies submit themselves to You. All the earth shall worship You and shall sing to You; they shall sing to Your name (Psalm 60:2-4).

O come ***let us worship and bow down, let us kneel before*** *the Lord our God,* and worship at His footstool, for He is Holy (Psalm 99:5). I will *sing to the Lord a new song.* I will bless Your name, and show forth Your salvation from day to day. I will declare Your glory among the heathen, Your wonders among the people. For You Lord are great, and greatly to be praised, You are to be feared above all gods (Psalm 96:1-4). For You have done marvelous things, Your right hand and Your holy arm has gotten You the victory (Psalm 98:1). I will sing of mercy and judgement to You, O Lord, will I sing. My lips shall praise You, thus will I bless You, while I live. I will *lift up my hands in Your name.* My mouth shall praise You with joyful lips (Psalm 63:3,4).

O *clap your hands* all you people, shout to God with the voice of triumph. The Lord Most High is terrible. You are a great King over all the earth (Psalm 47:1-2). I will *lift up my hands* in the sanctuary and bless You Lord (Psalm 134:2). Bless the Lord, O my soul, and all that is within me, bless His Holy name (Psalm 103:1). O Lord my God, You are very great, You are clothed with honour and majesty (Psalm 104:1). Praise Him with the sound of the trumpet. Praise Him with the psaltry and harp. *Praise Him with the timbrel and dance,* praise Him with stringed instruments and organs, praise Him upon the high sounding cymbals. Let everything that has breath praise the Lord (Psalm 150:3-5).

More Reasons for Thanks and Praise (personal)

Bless You O Lord because You have heard the voice of my supplication. Lord, You are my strength and my shield, my heart trusted in You, and I am helped. Therefore my heart greatly rejoices, and with my song I praise You (Psalm 28:6,7). I extol You, O Lord, for You have lifted me up, and have not made my foes to rejoice over me (Psalm 30:1). I bless the Lord at all times, Your praise shall continually be in my mouth (Psalm 34:1). I will not forget all Your benefits. You forgive all my iniquities, You heal all my diseases, You redeem my life from destruction and crown me with Your loving-kindness and tender mercies. You satisfy my mouth with good things, so that my youth is renewed like the eagle (Psalm 103:2-5). I praise You because I am fearfully and wonderfully made (Psalm 139:14).

My soul shall be satisfied as with marrow and fatness (Psalm 63:5). My soul is escaped as a bird out of the snare of the fowlers. The snare is broken, and I am escaped. My help is in the name of the Lord, who made the heaven and earth (Psalm 124:7,8). I will bless the Lord, You have given me counsel, my heart also instructs me in the night season (Psalm 16:7). You instruct me and teach me in the way which I should go. You guide me with Your eyes (Psalm 32:8), praise the Lord (Psalm 149:9).

Where to Praise

I will praise the Lord in the assembly of the upright (Psalm 111:1). I will praise You among the multitudes (Psalm 109:30). I will exalt You also in the congregation of the people and praise You in the assembly of the elders (Psalm 107:32).

When to Praise

Blessed be the Lord God from everlasting to everlasting (Psalm 41:1). Let my mouth be filled with Your praise and Your honour all the day long. I will hope continually, I will yet praise You more and more. My mouth shall show forth Your righteousness and Your salvation all the day for I know not the numbers thereof (Psalm 71:8,14,15). Blessed be

Your Name O Lord from this time forth and forevermore. From the rising of the sun to the going down of the same, the Name of the Lord is to be praised (Psalm 113:2,3).

Who Shall Praise

Teach me to number my days that I may apply my heart to wisdom (Ps. 90:12). You who fear the Lord, praise Him, all you seed of Jacob glorify Him, and fear Him all you seed of Israel. Those who seek Him will praise the Lord (Psalm 22:23,26). Praise Him O you servants of the Lord, you that stand in the house of the Lord, in the courts of the house of our God. Praise the Lord for the Lord is good. Sing praises to His Name for it is pleasant (psalm 135:1-3). Praise the Lord all you nations, praise Him all you people. For His merciful kindness is great toward us and the truth of the Lord endure forever (Psalm 117:1,2).

Let the heaven and earth praise Him, the seas and everything that moves in them (Psalm 69:34). Lord You are high above all nations, and Your glory. above the heavens. Who is like unto the Lord our God, who dwells on high (Psalm 113:4,5). Praise Him, all His angels, praise Him all His hosts. Praise Him sun and moon, praise Him, all stars and light. Praise Him, heavens of heavens, and you waters that be above the heavens. Let them praise the Lord for He commanded and they were created. He has also established them forever and ever. He has made a decree which shall not pass.

Praise the Lord from the earth, you dragons and all deeps. Fire and hail, snow and vapors, stormy wind fulfilling His word. Mountains, and all hills, fruitful trees, and all cedars, beaks and all cattle, creeping things and flying fowl, kings of the earth, and all people, princes, and all judges of the earth. Both young men and maidens, old men and children. Let them praise the Name of the Lord, for His Name alone is excellent, His glory is above the earth and heaven (Psalm 148:2-13). Let everything that has breath praise the Lord (Psalm 150:6). Let the people praise You, O God, Let the people praise You, then shall the earth yield her increase, and God even our God, shall bless us, and all the ends of the earth shall fear You (Psalm 67:5-7).

My Commitment to Praise

Open to me the gates of righteousness, I will go in to them, I will praise You Lord (Psalm 118:19). O Lord open my lips, and my mouth shall show forth Your praises (Psalm 51:15). I will praise You with uprightness of heart, when I shall have learned Your righteous judgments (Psalm 119:7). You are my God, and I will praise You. You are my God, and I will exalt You (Psalm 118:28). I will offer to You the sacrifices of thanksgiving and will call upon the Name of the Lord (Psalm 116:17). I will bind the sacrifice with cords even to the horns of the altar (Psalm 118:27).

Your vows are upon me, O God, I will render praise to You (Psalm 56:12). I will make Your Name to be remembered in all generations (Psalm 45:17), showing to the generations to come the praises of the Lord. I will not hide them from our children (Psalm 78:4). The upright shall dwell in Your presence (Psalm 140:13). Blessed is the man that fear the Lord, that delight greatly in His commandments (Psalm 112:1). My heart is fixed, O God, my heart is fixed. I will sing and give praise (Psalm 57:7). I will sing praise to Your Name forever, that I may daily perform my vows (Psalm 61:8). My God, my King, I bless Your Name forever and ever. Every day I will bless You. Great are You Lord and greatly to be praised, and Your greatness is unsearchable. I will speak of the glorious honour of Your majesty, and of Your wondrous works. I will declare Your greatness. Lord You are gracious, and full of compassion, slow to anger and of great mercy. Lord You are good to all, and Your tender mercies are over all Your works (Psalm 145:1,2,3,5,6,8,9). As the deer pants for the water brooks, so my soul longs for You, O God. My soul thirsts for God, for the living God (Psalm 42:1,2).

O that I may dwell in Your presence all the days of my life, to behold Your beauty Lord, and to inquire in Your presence (Psalm 27:4). In Your presence is fullness of Joy, at Your right hand are pleasures forevermore (Psalm 16:11). What shall I render to You Lord for all Your benefits towards me (Psalm 116:12). For You desire not sacrifices, else would I give it. The sacrifices of God are a broken spirit, a broken and a contrite heart, O God, You will not despise (Psalm 51:16,17). I will praise You forever and ever. I will wait upon Your Name for it is good (Psalm 52:9). Praise waits for You, O God, and unto You shall the vow be performed (Psalm 65:1).

2. From Psalm 119: The Fear of The Lord

O that my ways were direct to keep Your statutes, then shall I not be ashamed when I have respect to all Your commandments. I will praise You with uprightness of heart (v.5-7). Your word have I hid in my heart that I might not sin against You (v.11). I will meditate in Your Precepts and have respect to Your ways. I will delight myself in Your statutes (v.15,16). You have rebuked the proud that are cursed, which do err from Your commandments (v.21). I have chosen the way of truth (v.30). I will delight myself in Your commandments, which I have loved, my hands also will I lift up to Your commandments which I have loved and I will meditate in Your statutes (v.47,48). Horror had taken hold upon me because of the wicked that forsake Your law (v.53). I am a companion of all them that fear You and of them that keep Your precepts (v.63). They that fear You will be glad when they see me, because I hoped in Your Word (v.74). Let those that fear You turn to me and those that have known Your testimonies (v.79). O how I love. Your law, it is my meditation all the day (v.97). I have refrained my feet from every evil way that I may keep Your word (v.101). Through Your precepts I get understanding, therefore I hate every false way (v.104). I hate vain thoughts but Your law do I love (v.113). Depart from me you evil doers, for I will keep the commandments of my God (v.115). You have trodden down all them that err from Your statutes, for their deceit is falsehood. You put away all the wicked like dross, therefore I love Your testimonies. My flesh tremble for fear of You and I am afraid of Your judgments (v.118-120). It is time for the Lord to work, for they have made void Your law (v.126). I esteem all Your precept concerning all things to be right, and I hate every false way (v.128). Order my steps in Your word, and let not any iniquity have dominion over me (v.133). Rivers of waters run down my eyes because they do not keep Your law (v.136). My zeal has consumed me because my enemies have forgotten Your words (v.139). Your testimonies that You have commanded are righteous and very faithful (v.138). Your word is very pure, therefore Your servant loves it (v.140). Your righteousness is an everlasting righteousness and Your law is the truth (v.142). All Your commandments are truth (v.151). Salvation is far from the wicked, for they do not seek Your statutes (v.155). I beheld the transgressors and I was grieved because they did not keep Your word (v. 158). My heart stands in awe of Your word (v.161). I hate and abhor lying, but Your law do I love (v.163). Great peace have they which love Your law and nothing shall offend them (v.165).

My Relationship with the Word

I rejoice in the way of Your testimonies as much as in all riches (v.14). My soul breaks for the longing that it has to Your judgments at all times (v.20). Your testimonies are my delight and my counselors (v.24). I have chosen the way of truth; Your judgments have I laid before me (v.30). Behold I have longed after Your precepts (v.40). For I trust in Your word (v.42). I have hoped in Your judgments (v.43). I am a companion of all them that fear You, and of those who keep Your precepts (v.63). I delight in Your law (v.70). The law of Your mouth is better˜ to me than thousands of gold and silver (v.72). Forever, O Lord Your word is settled in heaven (v.89). O how I love Your law, it is my meditation all the day (v.97). You, through Your commandments, has made me wiser than my enemies, for they are ever with me (v.98). How sweet are Your words to my taste. Yes, sweeter than honey to my mouth (v.103). Your word is a lamp to my feet and a light to my path (v.105). Your testimonies have I taken as a heritage forever for they are the rejoicing of my heart (v.111). I hate vain thoughts, but Your law do I love (v.113). You are my hiding place and my shield, I hope in Your word (v.114). My flesh trembles for fear of You; and I am afraid of Your judgments (v. 120). I love Your commandments above gold; yes above fine gold (v.127). I esteem all Your precepts, concerning all things to be right, and I hate every false way (v.128). Your testimonies are wonderful; therefore my soul keeps them (v.129). The entrance of' Your words gives light, it gives understanding to the simple (v.130). Rivers of waters run down my eyes because they keep not Your law (v.136). Righteous are You, O Lord, and upright are Your judgments (v.137). Your testimonies that You have commanded are righteous and very faithful (v. 138). My zeal has consumed me because my enemies have forgotten Your words (v.139). Your word is very pure, therefore Your servant loves it (v.140). Your righteousness is an everlasting righteousness, and Your law is the truth (v.142). I beheld the transgressors and was grieved, because they did not keep Your word (v.158). Consider how I love Your precepts (v.159). Your words true from the beginning and every one of' Your righteous judgments endure forever (v.160). My heart stand in awe of Your word (v.161). I rejoice at Your word, as one that finds great spoil (v.162). I hate and abhor lying, but Your law I love (v.163). Seven times a day do I praise You because of Your righteous judgments (v.164). My soul has kept Your testimonies; and I love them exceedingly (v.167). I have kept Your precepts and Your testimonies for all my ways are before You (v.168). My lips shall utter praise when You have taught me Your statutes (v. 171). My tongue shall speak of Your word; for all Your commandments are righteousness (v.172). I have chosen Your precepts (v.173).

'But and Yet' Nevertheless I stay with the Word

Princes also did sit and speak against me, but Your servant did meditate on Your statutes (v.23). The proud have had me greatly in derision, yet I have not declined from Your law (v.51). The bands of the wicked have bound me, but I have not forsaken Your law (v.61). The proud have forged a lie against me, but I will keep Your precepts with my whole heart (v.69). Their heart is as fat as grease, but I delight in Your law (v.70). Let the proud be ashamed for they dealt perversely with me without cause, but I will meditate in Your precepts (v.78).

For I am become like a bottle in the smoke, yet I do not forget Your statutes (v.83). They had almost consumed me upon earth, but I forsook not Your precepts (v.87). The wicked have waited for me to destroy me, but I will consider Your testimonies (v.95). My soul is continually in my hand, yet do I not forget Your law (v.109). The wicked have laid a snare for me, yet I erred not from Your precepts (v.110). I am small and despised, yet I do not forget Your precepts (v·141). Many are my persecutors and mine enemies, yet I do not decline from Your testimonies (v.157). Princes have persecuted me without a cause, but my heart stands in awe of Your word (v.161).

I Make a Quality Decision

I will praise You with uprightness of heart when I shall have learned Your righteous judgments (v.7). I will keep Your statutes, forsake me not utterly (v.8). I will meditate on Your precepts and have respect to Your ways (v.15). I will delight myself in Your statues; I will not forget Your word (v.16). I will run the way of Your commandments when You enlarge my heart. Teach me O Lord the way of Your statutes and I shall keep it to the end. Give me understanding and I shall keep Your law, yea I shall keep it with my whole heart (v.33-34). I will walk at liberty for I seek Your precepts. Therefore, I will speak of Your testimonies also before kings and will not be ashamed. I will delight myself in Your commandments, which I have loved. My hands also will I lift up to Your commandments, which I have loved, and I will meditate on Your statutes (v.45-48). At midnight, I will rise to give thanks to You because of Your righteous judgments (v.62). The proud have forged a lie against me but I will keep Your precepts with my whole heart (v. 69). They that fear You will be glad when they see me because I have hoped in Your word (v.74). Let the proud be ashamed for they dealt perversely with me without a cause, but I will meditate on

Your precepts. Let those that fear You turn to me and those that know Your testimonies (v.78-79). I will never forget Your precepts for with them You have quickened me (v.93). The wicked have waited for me to destroy me but I will consider Your testimonies (v.95). I have sworn and I will perform it that I will keep Your righteous judgments (v.106). Depart from me you evil doers for I will keep the commandments of my God (v.115). Hold me up, and I shall be safe, and I will have respect to Your statutes continually (v.117). Deliver me from the oppression of man, so will I keep Your precepts (v.134). I cried with my whole heart, hear me O Lord, I will keep Your statutes. I cried to You save me, and I shall keep Your testimonies (v.145-146).

Prayer for Understanding

Open my eyes that I may behold wonderful things out of Your law (v.18). Give me understanding and I shall keep Your law. I shall observe it with my whole heart (v.34). Your hands have made me and fashioned me, give me understanding that I may learn Your commandments (v.73). I am Your servant, give me understanding that I may know Your testimonies (v.125). The righteousness of Your testimonies is everlasting, give me understanding and I shall live (v.144). Let my cry come near before You, o Lord, give me understanding according to Your word (v.169). I have more understanding than all my teachers, for Your testimonies are my meditation (v.99). I understand more than the ancients because I keep Your precepts (v.100). Through Your precepts I get understanding (v.104). The entrance of Your word gives light, it gives understanding to the simple (v.130).

Prayer for Personal Revival

Quicken me Lord according to Your Word (v.25). Turn away my eyes from vanity and quicken me in Your way (v.37). I long after Your precepts, quicken me in Your righteousness (v.40). This is my comfort in my affliction, for Your word has quickened me (v.50). Quicken me after Your loving-kindness so I keep the testimony of Your mouth (v.88). I will never forget Your precepts, for with them Thou has quickened me (v.93). I am afflicted very much, quicken me Lord according to Your word (v.107). Hear my voice according unto Your loving-kindness Lord, quicken me according to Your judgement (v.149). Plead my cause and deliver me, quicken me according to Your word (v.154). Great are Your tender mercies, O Lord; quicken me according to Your judgments (v.156). Consider how I love Your precepts. Quicken me Lord, according to Your loving-kindness (v.159).

Prayers from Psalm 119

Jesus said in John 16:23, *"And in that day you will ask Me nothing. Most assuredly, I say to you, whatever you ask the Father in My name He will give you."*

I pray in Jesus name;

that my ways were directed to keep Your statutes! (v.5). With my whole heart, I have sought You; Oh, let me not wander from Your commandments! (v.10). Deal bountifully with Your servant, That I may live and keep Your Word (v.17). Open my eyes, that I may see Wondrous things from Your law (v.18). I am a stranger in the earth; Do not hide Your commandments from me (v.19). Remove from me reproach and contempt (v.22). Revive me according to Your Word (v.25). Teach me Your statutes (v.26). Make me understand the way of Your precepts; So shall I meditate on Your wondrous works (v.27). Strengthen me according to Your Word (v.28). Remove from me the way of lying, And grant me Your law graciously (v.29). Do not put me to shame! (v.31). Teach me, O LORD, the way of Your statutes, And I shall keep it to the end. (v.33). Make me walk in the path of Your commandments, For I delight in it (v.35). Incline my heart to Your testimonies, And not to covetousness (v.36).

Turn away my eyes from looking at worthless things, And revive me in Your way (v.37). Establish Your Word to Your servant, Who is devoted to fearing You (v.38). Revive me in Your righteousness (v.40). Let Your mercies come also to me, O Lord; Even Your salvation according to Your word (v.41). And take not the Word of truth utterly out of my mouth (v.43) Remember the Word to Your servant, Upon which You have caused me to hope (v.49). I entreated Your favor with my whole heart; Be merciful to me (v.58). Teach me good judgment and knowledge (v.66). Let, I pray, Your merciful kindness be for my comfort (v.76). Let Your tender mercies come to me, that I may live; For Your law is my delight (v.77). Let the proud be ashamed (v.78). Let those who fear You turn to me as well as those who know Your testimonies (v.79). Let my heart be blameless.

Let my heart be sound in Your statues (v.80). When will You execute judgment on them that persecute me? (v.88). They persecute me wrongfully, help me (v.86). I am Yours, save me; for I have sought Your precepts (v.94). Uphold me according to Your Word, that I may live and let me not be ashamed of my hope (v.116). Hold me up and I shall be safe (v.117). Deal with me your servant according to Your mercies and teach me Your statutes (v.124). Look upon me and be merciful to me, as You used to do to them that love Your name (v.132). Order my steps in Your Word, and let not any iniquity have dominion over me (v.133). Deliver me from the oppression of man, so will I keep Your precepts (v.134). I will refrain my feet from every evil way, that I might keep Your word (v.101). Make Your face to shine upon me Your servant, and teach me Your statutes (v.135). Hear my voice according to Your loving kindness (v.149). Consider my affliction and deliver me, for I do not forget Your law (v.153). Plead my cause and deliver me (v.154). Quicken me, O Lord, according to Your loving kindness (v.159). Let my soul live, and it shall praise You and let Your judgment help me (v.175). Let me not go astray like a lost sheep; seek Your servant for I do not forget Your commandments (v.176).

I ask these things in Jesus' name and I receive them based on Jesus' shed blood, on the mercy seat. 1 receive them with thanksgiving in the name of Jesus Christ my Lord and Saviour. Amen!

Section II: *Confessions*

H. Short Confessions

"You shall also decree a thing, and it shall be established for you" **(Job 22:28).**

Miscellaneous Confessions

1. I am living in perpetual prosperity in every area of my life because I delight myself in the law of the Lord and in His law I do meditate day and night. I am like a tree planted by the rivers of water that brings forth fruit in its seasons. My leaf shall not wither and whatever I do prospers (Psalm 1:2-3).

2. I am utterly ruled and governed by the Word of God and the Holy Spirit so that I am becoming a master of demons and their work. I cast out demons with the Word. I pray for the sick and diseases leave them. The very life of God flows through my lips (Mark 16:17,18,20).

3. I am a labourer together with God (2 Corinthians 6:1).

4. I believe as a child of God and joint heir with Jesus. I can walk in the same life, power and divine liberty as Jesus walked, as I understand and appropriate my privileges (Romans 8:11; 1 John 4:17).

5. I am determined to walk in the fullness of the new creation life (Ephesians 4:22-24).

6. I humbly and fearlessly in the name of the Lord Jesus Christ take my place as a son of God (Romans 8:19).

7. I am what God says I am. He is in what He says He is. I can do with His ability in me what He says I can (Philemon 6; Philippians 4:13).

8. The greater One is in me. I am linked up with ability and omnipotence (1 John 4:4).

9. The very character of God and the nature of God is being built into my life through the Word. It is no longer I that live but Christ lives in me (Ephesians 5:26-27; Galatians 2:20).

10. In the name of Jesus I am an absolute master of satan and demons (Luke 6:10-19).

11. God has imparted his own nature, eternal life, to me. I am a new man, over whom satan has no dominion (1 John 5:11-12; Romans 6:14).

12. I am free, the Son has made me free, and I am free in reality (John 8:36).

13. I thank You Father that when I pray in the name of Jesus You always hear me (John 16:23).

14. I am the very righteousness of God Himself. I have the ability to stand in the Father's presence without condemnation or inferiority (2 Corinthians 5:21; Hebrews 10:19).

15. The Word is a part of the Father Himself. I feed on the Word. I breathe the Word into my spirit. The Word of God is being built into my spirit-consciousness (John 1:1; John 15:16).

16. I walk by faith and not by sight (2 Corinthians 5:7).

17. I confess I have dominion over disease in Jesus' name (Matthew 10:1).

18. I cannot be conquered. My God and I are masters of every situation. In all these things I am more than a conqueror (2 Corinthians 2:14; Romans 8:37).

19. I have learned in whatever state I am in to be independent of circumstances (Philippians 4:11).

20. I never talk failure; I never talk defeat. God's ability can and will put me over (Psalm 17:34).

21. I am God-inside of me minded (Romans 8:6,9).

22. God has blessed me with every spiritual blessing in Christ (Ephesians 1:3).

23. All things are mine (1 Corinthians 3:1).

24. Jehovah is my Light and my Salvation. Whom shall I fear? Jehovah is the strength of my life. I shall not be afraid (Psalm 27:1).

25. I am a partaker of Christ's resurrection (Colossians 3:1).

26. The Father has given me the ability He exercised in the resurrection of Jesus (Ephesians 1:19-20).

27. I have in my possession the resurrection power of God which is the ability of God (Ephesians 3:20).

28. The mighty One is in me. He can put me over today so that I can face any emergency. I can do all things in Him because He is my strength (Philippians 4:13).

29. Jesus is all that I need. He is my helper, my wisdom, my strength and my ability (Colossians 1:29; 1 Corinthians 1:30). Nothing is impossible with God (Matthew 19:26), and nothing shall be impossible for me (Matthew 17:20). All things that I pray and ask for, believing I will receive them, I shall have them (Mark 11:24). All things are possible to me because I am a believing one.

30. All authority in Heaven and on earth is invested in the name of Jesus (Matthew 28:18).

31. Failure has no place in my life. I have God's unlimited ability. I can do all things (Philippians 4:13).

32. Father you laid every sickness and disease on Jesus, and it is not appropriate for me to bear any sickness. I would dishonour you by bearing it. So in the name of Jesus, I command sickness to go from me. I forbid satan from afflicting me with any sickness or disease, and I command my body to dwell in divine health. I refuse to allow sickness in my body or my home in the name of Jesus.

33. Jesus is my sufficiency. There is no lack in me. For the Lord is my shepherd, I shall not want. He is my provision and sufficiency (Psalm 23:1).

34. I am blessed with everything I need. His very fullness is mine. His ability is mine. His love is mine. He Himself is mine (Ephesians 1:3; Colossians 2:9,10).

35. I am a channel through which God pours Himself upon the world. It is perfectly normal that He should become my sufficiency, that His ability should become my ability. I am made one with Omnipotence

(2 Corinthians 3:5; 2 Corinthians 4:7).

36. I am God's transmitter. We are labourers together. My lips, hands, and body are available for His use. I am sanctified and purged by the Word. So now I can bring him glory, producing much fruit (2 Corinthians 6:1; John 15:3-9).

37. His Words in my lips make me a supernatural man (Jeremiah 5:14).

38. His love has been delegated to me. His love pours through my lips.

39. I am not only a new creation and a son, but I am also a partner in His work of bringing His redemption to humanity. We are workers together. I am the fruit bearing part of the company (John 15:5).

40. God, my Father, has created me, imparting His own nature, eternal life, to me. Now I stand before Him as though I have never sinned, been weak, been a failure, or been under condemnation. I am now His righteousness. I am a man of faith and power (2 Peter 1:4; 2 Corinthians 5:21).

41. I am born of Heaven. My citizenship is there. I have received my credentials from Heaven (Philippians 3:20).

42. Whatever I ask in Jesus' name He makes good (John 16:23).

43. It is with the Word I have to do (Hebrews 4:12-13). I contact God through the Word and God contacts

me through the Word. I act on the Word.

44. I need to see myself as the Father sees me in Christ. As He sees me by faith, He is able to make me by grace. As I walk in faith and love, I am being transformed into His image (2 Corinthians 3:18).

45. Love is at work within me, willing and working His own good pleasure (Philippians 2:13).

46. I am of love, for God is love, and have overcome them...because greater is love in me than selfishness, hatred and jealousy around me (1 John 4:4).

47. I am in love and love reigns in me. God and I have become one in love. Now His love life is pouring through me, blessing and helping me (1 Corinthians 6:17).

48. My secret is the fact that I visit almost continuously with my Father of love, faith, and power.

49. I am consumed with the desire and determination to please my Father.

50. I am ever ready to distribute and willing to communicate. I am a giver and a tither (1 Timothy 6:18).

51. God, my Father loves me and He will do me good (John 17:23; Psalms 84:11).

52. I do not allow anxiety to govern me in anything at anytime. But in everything by prayer and supplication, along with thanksgiving, I make my requests known to the Father. Then I leave them

there. I declare that His peace will come like a battalion of soldiers into a turbulent country and quiet me and keep my mind and soul in perfect peace (Philippians 4:6,7).

53. God's fullness takes me over and dominates me. His fullness of love, grace, wisdom, peace, healing and ability has displaced all the weakness and failures that existed in my life. I practice the presence of God (Psalm 16:8).

54. The devil, demons or circumstances cannot fill me with doubt and fear because I know in whom I have believed and I am resting in His grace (2 Timothy 1:12).

55. I am a new creation, a partaker of the very nature of the Father. I have received the Father's overflowing grace, and the gift of righteousness, and now I reign as a king in this new realm of life (2 Corinthians 5:17; Romans 5:17).

56. The secret of faith is the secret of confession (Matthew 17:20).

57. Every time I break the silence caused by fear with an open confession of the integrity of the Word, and I act on the Word, I destroy the very roots of fear and unbelief in my life.

58. A wrong confession hinders the Spirit's work in my life (Galatians 3:5).

59. The Son has made me free and I am free indeed. I stand fast in that liberty (John 8:36; Galatians 5:1).

60. My Father is for me (Romans 8:31).

61. God is at work within me, willing, and working His own good pleasure (Philippians 2:13).

62. I confess that God lives in me and ministers through me (John 14:10).

63. Jesus is my Intercessor and He ever lives to stand for me. The secret of my success and victory is His continual intercession and His enablement (Hebrews 7:25).

64. Jesus is my wisdom. He is the strength of my life (1 Corinthians 1:30).

65. Satan has no ability to break the seal of the blood. By the Blood of Christ and the Word of God. I overcome the enemy (Revelation 12:11).

66. The Lord is my helper. I do not want (Psalm 27:1).

67. I must not allow any kind of pressure or circumstances to cause me to change my confession. My confession must be based entirely on God, His Word, His nature, His character, His promises, His faithfulness, His power, His love, the Blood of Jesus, and Jesus' high priest ministry. I must look at Jesus and unto Jesus, keeping my eyes on Him. This means I must look away from circumstances, contradictions, man's opinions, etc. I must walk by the eye of faith focused on Jesus and not by sight (2 Corinthians 4:18; Hebrews 12:1; 2 Corinthians 5:7).

68. I live in the overflow of the presence, the glory and

the goodness of God. I practice the presence of God (Psalms 16:11).

69. Money comes to me now for the glory of God and the establishment of His covenant in my life, family and in the earth (Deuteronomy 8:18).

70. The Word of God is like a fire in my month accomplishing the purposes of God. It brings refreshment to believers and judgement on sinners (Jeremiah 5:14).

71. Being made free from sin, I have become a servant of righteousness. I have my fruit unto holiness and the end everlasting life (Romans 6:18,22).

72. I expect miracles! (Mark 16:17,20).

73. I am the temple of God. God dwells in me and walks with me (2 Corinthians 6:16).

74. I have the victory over death through my Lord Jesus Christ (I Corinthians 15:57).

75. The Word of God is the Father speaking to me.

76. There is nothing I cannot have, nothing I cannot do, nowhere I cannot go, nothing I cannot be, because God is on the inside. His Word is working in me.

77. Lord, I expect miracles to take place in my life today, miracles in my family, body, and finances. I expect miracles in my life and ministry.

78. My words have authority, ability and power.

79. I live in the realm where nothing is impossible, because I am hooked up with an omnipotent, omniscient God (Matthew 19:26; Mark 19:23).

80. I am in Christ and Christ is in me. The works that I do are the works of Christ for it is Christ in me that do the works (John 14:10,11). Whatsoever I shall ask and demand in Jesus' name He will do it (John 14:13).

81. Whatever I talk to has to obey me just like it would obey Jesus. I have the same spirit of faith (2 Corinthians 4:13).

82. I am full of confidence and boldness and the Spirit of faith.

83. My Father is omnipresent and His banner over me is love.

Financial Confessions

1. God meets my every need and I have an abundant supply.

2. The Lord Who is my Shepherd is taking me higher into new realms of financial prosperity.

3. It is God's good will and pleasure to prosper me.

4. I will never be broke. I plead the Blood of Jesus over my finances.

5. God is my Father and has provided for me to have

prosperity.

6. Debt, go from me in Jesus' name.

7. Curse, get out of my way. Prosperity, come my way.

8. Prosperity comes my way now (Psalm 118:25).

9. God helps me get out of debt because I am redeemed from poverty. I am coming into my inheritance.

10. I am at the top. I am rising above the world's system and am entering into the prosperity that God has provided for me. I am in covenant with God, and I am financing the preaching of the Gospel to every creation. Money comes to me.

11. I have a righteous attitude toward the Word of God. I have a right attitude toward the work of God. I have a giving attitude and a good attitude about tithing.

12. Satan, take your hands off my finances. I am not going to cooperate with you. Prosperity is mine, and I am going to receive what is mine in the name of Jesus. Money comes to me.

13. I am blessed exceedingly abundantly above all that I ask or think. There shall not be room enough to receive it (Malachi 3:10).

14. The Lord is bringing me into a good land. Money comes.

15. God does not want me living in scarceness or to lack any good thing. Money comes.

Section II - Confessions

16. Beginning now, my income is multiplying. Satan, take your hands off my finances. I do not believe your lies anymore. God does not want me, His child, in poverty. Poverty, get away from me. God wants me to prosper, and I am in agreement with God from this time forward. Hallelujah, money comes.

17. I believe God can get the money to me. Money comes to me now.

18. I claim the multiplied blessings of Deuteronomy 8:13. My silver and gold are multiplied. Money comes.

19. I see myself out of debt. I picture myself prosperous.

20. The power to get wealth is in me and that power is working in me continually.

21. Money comes to me because my Father said so. Therefore there will be no lack for preaching the Gospel or in my personal affairs. I am not covetous with the Lord's blessing, but I am a covenant partner with the plan, purpose and will of God.

22. God is my source and supplier. Therefore, I will always have more than enough. Money is not my master. Jesus is my master. I master and manage my money according to the will of God. Money comes to me.

23. I think the thoughts of God about wealth. I resist poverty, doubt and any suggestion of failure. I yield to the power of God in me to get wealth by thinking God's thoughts, confessing right and continuing to give tithes and offering in obedience to God. I resist the devil in thought, word and deed.

24. Jesus is my salvation, my rock, my deliverer and my financier.

25. My Father's name is El-Shaddai. He is the God Who is more than enough. His name is Jehovah-Jireh. He is my provider.

26. Father, my mind is made up. I am free from poverty. I am redeemed from poverty. Wallet, you are full of money in Jesus' name. I am going to get the Gospel preached with my finances. Devil, you are a liar. You have been lying to me. My Father wants me to have abundance, and I have abundance. I do not care what anyone else says about it. I only care what my Father says. I do not feel guilty for having plenty. Money comes to me.

27. Father, I thank You that You have given me seed to sow. I am a tither and a giver. I support and favour your righteous cause. I give to the Gospel. I tithe, give offering, listen to the spirit of God and give where God tells me to give. I am in partnership with several ministries that preach the Gospel and give to the poor. I participate in giving and receiving. I therefore have a Heavenly bank account. I therefore, humbly and boldly claim that Philippians 4:19 belongs to me, and You shall supply my every need according to your riches in glory by Christ Jesus. Father, I thank you for channeling money to me. Money comes to me.

28. The blessing of the Lord makes me rich and adds no sorrow with it. The blessing of the Lord crowns me with glory and honour and majesty. You have made me exceedingly glad with Your presence. Joy fills my

heart. I trust in You wholeheartedly. I rely and depend on You completely. I believe in You entirely. You are the Lord of Hosts. I humble myself in Your sight. I receive the peace that comes from the wholeness Your salvation brings because of Your mercy and loving-kindness (Proverbs 10:22; Psalm 21:5-7; Psalm 17:7)

29. I give to the church and the Gospel and fruit abounds to my account.

30. I am going to make it. I am going to prosper like God wants me to prosper. I am not going to hide my blessings.

31. My Father desires for me to have days of Heaven on the earth, so I will have days of Heaven on the earth (Deuteronomy 11:21)

32. I serve a Holy God. I am of the crowd that has integrity, intelligence and a spirit of excellence in all things,

33. I claim my blessings and I walk in divine prosperity. I do not pay any attention to the persecutions.

34. I do not have a corrupt mind. I have God and His Word. I do not love money.

35. I am not afraid of money. God gives me money to serve me and to serve God. Money is not my master. Jesus is my master.

36. Money is not evil, the love of money is evil. I need money to operate and I will have it. Money comes. I have it now.

37. Faith causes me to come into prosperity. I can handle money, success and prosperity. I do not think of myself more highly than I ought to think. It is God Who gives me the power to get wealth. It is God Who is prospering me. I receive my prosperity by faith. It is of faith that it might be according to grace. Therefore, my only boasting is in God, not myself.

38. As I enter into financial prosperity, I continue to trust in the living God and I do not let my trust be in money or uncertain riches.

39. I pay my bills and I have money left over because money comes and I walk in God's covenant of prosperity and peace that comes from being whole.

40. Christ has redeemed me from the curse of the law and money comes to me.

41. I have the revelation because I am in Christ, everything that the Father owns on the earth is mine.

42. I will not think poverty and lack. All things are mine.

43. I must always remember to keep God first and have the attitude that God owns everything. I own nothing. The things that I have, God is letting me use.

44. Jesus, You are my Lord and my Master. I yield everything I have to you—my home, my cars, my bank accounts, my talents, and my family. The world will not use what I have, Lord, because I yield it all to you.

45. I love God and according to Proverbs 8:21, God will cause me to inherit substance and fill my treasures.

46. God will fill my house with glory, His presence and gold.

47. I am prospering in Jesus' name. I am coming out of debt. I plead the Blood of Jesus over my situation. Jesus is bringing me out. Glory to God! There is no more bondage for me. Thank God almighty, I am free at last.

48. Poverty, you are under my feet. I am going on with prosperity unashamedly. Prosperity is not wrong. It is right. Tradition has lied to me. My prosperity is paid for. Jesus Christ has paid for it, and I am going to have it.

49. Prosperity belongs to the body of Christ, and I am part of the body of Christ. Therefore I am prosperous. I am coming out of debt. I am not going to barely get by. My Father says I should have more than enough, and I am going to have it.

50. The Lord is my Shepherd. He prepares a table before me in the presence of my enemies. He anoints my head with oil, my cup runs over with blessings. Money comes! God is opening the windows of heaven for me. He meets my every need according to His riches in glory by Christ Jesus. He is causing men to give to me good measure, pressed down, shaking together, and running over.

51. My prosperity is paid for. Money comes.

52. I am coming out of debt. Bills, you are paid, never to

haunt me again.

53. The wealth of the sinner is laid up for the just—that is me. The wealth of the sinner comes to me because God says so. Money comes (Proverbs 13:22).

54. I am a money magnet and money comes to me.

55. God daily loads me with benefits.

56. I access the grace and sufficiency of God in whatever area I need to by faith. My faith works because I have heard from God, and I have his Word on the subject.

57. God loves me perfectly, completely and unconditionally.

58. Grace abounds toward me.

59. I am full of power by the Spirit of God.

60. Goodness and mercy follow me wherever I go and all the days of my life.

61. I am empowered to prosper, increase and multiply in goods, silver, gold, houses, lands, money, and all that I have. God has given me the power to get wealth and increase and multiply in all things.

62. Prosperity pursues and overtakes me, the righteous.

63. Just enough is not enough.

64. I have millionaire status on the inside of me.

65. I have what it takes to be wealthy. It is part of my covenant inheritance.

66. Faith makes me talk like God. Faith gives me the right to talk like God.

67. To be broke and stay broke is dishonouring to the Blood of Jesus. It is the will of God that I prosper. Money comes to me now.

68. I have a legal and spiritual right to be rich.

69. I make demands on money and money obeys me. Money comes to me now for the glory of God and the establishment of His covenant with me and in the earth.

70. Supernatural income, increase, prosperity, favour and empowerment to prosper is upon me now.

71. God is my rapidly increasing money supply.

72. Wealth is being manifested on the inside of me now.

73. Angels are attending to me and my family. They are working on my behalf throughout the world wherever my influence is needed. Thank you, Lord.

Love Confessions

1. Surely goodness and mercy shall follow me all the days of my life (Psalm 23:6).

2. Father God in Heaven, I commit myself today to

develop in faith and in Your love. I commit myself to Your Word, to be pleasing to You, and to walk in love even as Jesus walked. I make a quality decision now to walk in love, talk in love, think in love, and to respond to all things in love. I renounce selfishness in the name of Jesus. It has no part in me. I am born of love, so I will walk in love.

3. I suffer long and I am kind. I do not envy. I am not puffed up. I do not behave unseemingly. I do not seek my own. I am not easily provoked. I think no evil. I do not rejoice in iniquity, but I rejoice in the truth. I bear all things, believe all things, hope all things, endure all things. I never fail.

4. I am a believer. I am born of love. The love way is my way because it is God's way and I am born of God.

5. I receive the commandment of love as a commandment.

6. My Lord Jesus came that men might have life more abundantly. As He is, so am I in this world. God sees me as He is in this world. Therefore as God's servant, I am here that men might have life more abundantly.

New Creation Confessions

1. I have the spirit of prayer and supplication, and I yield to it continually and daily in Jesus' name (Zechariah 12:10; Romans 8:15).

2. I walk after my born again spirit and thus I do not

fulfill the desires of my flesh and carnal nature (Galatians 5:16)

3. As I walk and live in the Spirit, I am responsive to, controlled by and guided by the Holy Spirit. I do not have the cravings and desires of the flesh.

4. I have in Him my victory over prayerlessness.

5. I am a master of confession.

6. I have what I say, my confession is my profession (Hebrews 3:1; Hebrews 4:14).

7. My mouth speaks truth and wickedness is an abomination to my lips (Proverbs 8:7).

8. I do not let the Word of God depart from before my eyes for it is life to me. I have found the Word, and it is health and healing to all my flesh (Proverbs 6:21-22).

9. The Word of God will not depart out of my mouth. I will meditate therein day and night. I observe to do according to all that is written therein. I am making my way prosperous and having good success (Joshua 1:8).

10. I am a believer, I am not a doubter.

11. I have received abundance of grace and the gift of righteousness. I am coming up higher and reigning in life by Jesus Christ (Romans 5:17; Revelation 4:1).

12. I see myself the way God, my Father, sees me. I am the righteousness of God in Christ (2 Corinthians

5:21). I am blessed with every spiritual blessing in Christ (Ephesians 1:13). I am free from condemnation, guilt, shame, inferiority and limitations (Romans 8:1; Hebrews 9:14). I can do all things through Christ who strengthens me (Philippians 4:13).

13. I am complete and entire in Christ, lacking nothing (Colossians 2:10).

14. I am found blameless in Christ. I have boldness before the throne of my Father God (Hebrews 10:19).

15. I am a master, a ruler, and a king in Christ (Romans 5:17a). I dominate my environment, devils, and demons.

16. God always causes me to triumph in Christ.

17. No weapon formed against me shall prosper because my righteousness is of God. I know no failure. I am free from my past and I only know success and victory in Christ (Isaiah 54:17; 2 Corinthians 2:14; Hebrews 8:12; 2 Corinthians 5:18; 1 Corinthians 15:57).

18. I have no shortage of power or anointing. Christ in me is the hope of glory. Christ is the power and wisdom of God in me. Greater is He that is in me than he that is in the world (Colossians 1:27; 1 John 4:4).

19. God sees me as strong and great (Isaiah 53:12) and rich (1 Timothy 6:17; 2 Corinthians 8:9); and I see

me the way God does.

20. I am a son of God, and I am led by the Spirit of God (Romans 8:14).

21. I am established, fixed, and settled in the righteousness of God in Christ. I do not fear and I shall not fear. I am therefore free from oppression, and from terror, it shall not come near me (Isaiah 54:17). God has declared and made me righteous by His grace through the power of the resurrection. I am an heir according to the hope of eternal life, the perpetuation of the God life (Titus 3:7).

22. The Holy Spirit of God is within me, upon me, and around me. I live in the atmosphere of the Holy Spirit.

23. I am anointed by God. I am anointed to praise, to preach, to teach, to heal the sick, and to set the captives free. I am anointed to restore truth to the human race. I am anointed to be a tree of righteousness planted by the Lord. I am anointed to walk in joy and praise.

24. The anointing in me teaches me all things. The anointing in me is my wisdom and the power of God. I can do all things through the anointing that enables me.

25. I yield to the anointing within me, therefore I am healed, prosperous and free from the curse.

26. Christ is to me all that I could ever need. Christ is made unto me wisdom, strength, righteousness and sanctification. Christ is the strength and health of my entire being, spirit, soul and body. Christ is my

hope, my confidence, my present and my future. Christ is being fully formed in me now. Praise be to God (Colossians 3:11; 1 Corinthians 1:30; Colossians 1:27; Colossians 3:4; Galatians 4:19).

27. Christ is the grace and ability from God in me to give me an effective prayer life, a life of discipline and a spirit controlled life.

28. I am an able minister of the Gospel and the new covenant, because Christ in me is my sufficiency (2 Corinthians 12:9; 1 Corinthians 3:5-6).

29. As He is, so am I in this world (1 John 4:17).

Prayer Life Confessions

1. I walk in the spirit, therefore, I pray constantly. Because I pray constantly, I remain in the Spirit.

2. I take time to pray and talk with the Lord for at least one hour every day. I spend time in the Word every day. I pray in the spirit constantly. I meditate in the Word day and night. My confession is my profession. I am a doer of the Word, not a hearer only.

3. Prayerlessness is sin and where sin abounds grace abounds much more. The spirit of grace, prayer and supplication reigns through righteousness producing eternal life. The perpetual life of God manifests in me the spirit crying out through me, Abba Father. Prayerlessness flows out of sin consciousness, producing death. But thanks be to God who gives me the victory of prayerfulness,

flowing out of righteous consciousness, and producing the fruit of righteousness—the manifestation of the perpetual life of God (1 Samuel 12:23).

4. Prayerlessness will not have dominion over me, for I am not under the law but under grace (1 Samuel 12:23; Romans 5:20; Zechariah 12:10; Romans 5:21; Romans 8:15; Romans 7:23-29; Romans 8:26; Romans 6:23, Romans 6:14; Philippians 1:11)

5. I walk as Christ is in me living through me.

6. I walk and live in the consciousness of being one with God.

7. Thank God I am the righteousness of God in Christ. Jesus is in me and living through me.

8. I belong to Christ. I was raised up together with Him. They that are Christ's have crucified the flesh with the affections, passions, and lusts. I have therefore crucified the flesh with its passions and lust according to the revelation of God's Word and the faith of the operation of God. (Galatians 5:24; Colossians 2:12).

9. I am dead to the world and the world is dead to me. I am dead to the lust of the flesh, the lust of the eyes, and the pride of life, and they are dead to me. I command the world, the flesh, and ungodly passions to be silent. I am dead to you and you are dead to me. Do not talk to me or even try to get my attention in Jesus' name.

10. I am alive to God. The Word of God is working effectually in me bringing soundness and salvation

to my entire being, spirit, soul and body.

11. My heart is good soil for the Word of God. The Word of God produces in me one hundred fold profusely.

12. I walk and live in the consciousness of the presence of God being in me, on me, and around me in Jesus' name by faith.

Minister's Confessions

1. So greatly grew the Word of the Lord and prevailed (Acts 1:20).

2. The Word of the Lord grew and multiplied (Acts 12:24).

3. The harvest truly is plentiful. The Lord of the harvest is sending out labourers into His harvest (Matthew 9:37-38).

4. The Lord has sent us to reap where we did not bestow any labour. Other men laboured and we have entered into their labour (John 4:38).

5. I believe there is supernatural increase in the ministry and every aspect of ministry outreach in Jesus' name.

6. The Lord is increasing us more and more, and our children also. We are blessed of the Lord who made heaven and earth (Psalm 115:14-15).

7. The ministry activities are empowered by God to prosper and increase in the knowledge of God

(Deuteronomy 8:18; Colossians 1:10).

8. Grace and peace is multiplied toward us through the knowledge of God. We are blessed and surrounded with favour as a shield. All grace and favour is abounding toward us (2 Peter 1:2; Psalm 5:12; 2 Corinthians 9:8).

9. My God is supplying all our need according to His riches in glory by Christ Jesus. Blessed be the name of the Lord. I rejoice and shout for joy. Our trust is in Him (Philippians 4:19; Psalm 5:11).

10. Father God, I thank you for impregnating my words with Yourself so that when I speak, I speak as an oracle of God and my words are filled with power, spirit and life, even the Word of God so that men are able to receive and accept it not as the word of men, but as it is in reality, the Word of God which works in them that believe (John 12:50; 1 Peter 4:11; John 6:63; 1 Thessalonians 2:13).

11. I confess I am a son of God and a servant of the Lord. I am come to carry out my part in the Great Commission to make disciples of Christ of all nations. And to expose the lies of the enemy, show God's people their sins and transgressions and prepare the way of the Lord and to make people ready for Jesus' return.

12. Jesus in me is the authority over demonical forces and over the laws of nature.

13. I am a new man after God created in righteousness and holiness

14. Everything that Jesus did is accredited to me. The entire substitution work of Christ was for me. Every demon knows that in the name of Jesus I am his master. They can only rule us recreated ones by bluff, deception or ignorance

15. My Father who cannot lie says "If I abide in Christ and His Words abide in me, I can ask whatsoever I will and it shall be done to me (brought into being)." Furthermore He is glorified when I bring forth much fruit, prayer fruit, and answers to prayer (John 15:7-8).

16. I am the branch bearing prayer fruit. His righteousness is mine for He was made to me righteousness. I have become through the new birth, the very righteousness of God in Christ. My righteousness is just as good as Jesus' righteousness is. No one has better righteousness than I.

17. The Word is mine. The Holy Spirit is mine. Jesus is mine. God is my Father. Their righteousness is my righteousness. I stand complete in their completeness. I am a new creation created in Christ Jesus. All the rights and privileges of a child are mine. I did not have to ask for them. They were bestowed on me. When I became His child, these things were a part of the new creation, so I enter into my rights.

18. Just as demons, disease, physical needs and financial needs are subject to Jesus, they are likewise subject to me in the name of Jesus. In His name I cast out demons and rule over satan and his works.

19. I have the power of authority to use the name of

Jesus. All authority in Heaven and earth are wrapped up in the name of Jesus. Jesus has given me legal right to use His name.

20. Now I can destroy the works of the adversary. I can set men free. Now I can break the power and dominion of disease and demons over the bodies, hearts and minds of men. I can actually take Jesus' place and do His works. The works that Jesus did I will do also and greater works than those because He has gone to the Father. I have His own Word for it. I have the same spirit that raised Jesus from the dead within me. I have the same righteousness that Jesus had for He is that righteousness. I rejoice in the fact of satan's defeat. I have the name of Jesus. God is my own Father. What more can I ask. I am His own child. I am born of His own spirit, will, and plan. I am a partaker of His nature, eternal life. His Word has given me absolute assurance of my relationship with Him. So, fearlessly I make my confession to the world. I am a child of God. I am a new creation, heir of God, and joint heir with Jesus Christ. He loves me even as He loved Jesus. His home is my home. If Jesus tarries, I will go to my Father' home, for it is my home. These facts thrill my soul and give birth to and seal faith in my own heart. I have confidence in my faith. I know that whatsoever I ask the Father in Jesus' name, He will give it to me. I know I have authority over all the authority of the enemy in Jesus' name. I know I can come in confidence to my Father's throne of grace any time, day and night, and have His listening ear and gracious hand.

21. I am the Father's will. It is easy for me to do His will for I am born of it. I have His nature in me. I have

the impulses of His own love heart throbbing through me.

22. I am a partaker of God's nature. I have in me His faith nature. This makes me a child of faith. I have been begotten of the living Word through the Holy Spirit. The real me was created in Christ. I have the very nature of the Father and the Father is love, so I have in me the love nature of the Father.

23. I live in the Father's will.

24. I am a branch of the vine, and the same life and love that flows in the vine is in me.

25. I know whatsoever I ask the Father in Jesus' name He will give it to me.

26. The mighty Holy Spirit Who has come to make His home in my body is guiding me into the reality of the wealth that has been given to me in Christ.

Reminder: Speak the confessions and prayers out loud whenever possible. Faith comes by hearing and hearing the Word of God from your own lips.

Section III

Prayers

"And he spake a parable unto them to this end, that men ought always to pray, and not to faint" **(Luke 18:1).**

Section III: *Prayers*

A. General Prayers

"The earnest (heartfelt, continued) prayer of a righteous man makes tremendous power available [dynamic in its working]" (James 5:16b).

Prayer Guide Based on the Lord's Prayer
Matthew 6:9-15

If you were to go jogging, it would be a sensible idea to map your jogging course ahead of time, and plan how much time you would spend jogging. Jesus said, *"men ought always to pray."* You should pray whenever the Spirit of the Lord calls you to pray. You should also pray whenever the need arises. But it is also important to pray at specific, set times. Psalm 5:3 says, *"My voice shall you hear in the morning O Lord. In the morning will I direct my prayers unto you, and watch and wait for you to speak to my heart."*

It is most helpful to have a prayer outline that is Word-centered and one that includes praise, worship and submits to the leading of the Holy Spirit. The Lord's Prayer in Matthew 6:9-15 is one of many useful prayer outlines. Here it is broken down in a way that can help you to pray from ten minutes to ten hours.

"After this manner therefore pray" (Matthew 6:9):

Step 1:

Enter the presence of God, your Father by exercising faith in the Blood of Christ and giving thanks to God for the great benefits of your salvation. Study the following verses: Hebrews 10:19, Ephesians 3:12, and Psalm 100:4.

"Our Father who are in heaven..."

Praise God for Him being your Father and for you being His very own child. Rejoice because you have valid citizenship in Heaven (Philippians 3:20).

"Hallowed be Your Name..."

Worship, reverence and praise God based on His various names. Take time to study and reflect on the implication of His names to you personally.

Examples:

1. **Jehovah Tsidkenu - The Lord of Righteousness** (Jeremiah 23:6)
   Jesus became sin for you and you are now the righteousness of God in Christ (2 Corinthians 5:21). You are able to stand before God, in all His holiness, without any sense of guilt, condemnation, insecurity or inferiority. You are in right standing with God, having rights and authority as a son or daughter of God. You have fellowship with God and partake of His divine nature (2 Peter 1:4).

2. **Jehovah Shalom - The Lord is Peace** (Judges 6:24).
   Jesus is your peace, wholeness and completeness (Colossians 1:20). Praise God that the Blood of Christ testifies from the mercy seat of God (Hebrews 12:24) that you are complete in Christ (Colossians 2:10).

3. **Jehovah Raphé - The Lord our Healer** (Exodus 15:26)
   Jesus bore your sickness and carried your diseases (Matthew 8:17) so that you wouldn't have to bear them. By His stripes you were healed (1 Peter 2:24). Praise God because the stripes on Jesus' back and the blood that gushed out, declares your legal right to live in divine health. In the same way you have a right for sin

not to rule over you. (Romans 6:14). So rejoice before God and proclaim that you believe what the blood speaks. Healing belongs to you. The Spirit of God that raised Jesus from the dead is at work within you right now. Faith is now (Hebrews 11:1), energizing, empowering, and quickening your mortal body (Romans 8:11, Philippians 2:13).

4. **Jehovah-Jireh – The Lord sees, the Lord provides** (Genesis 22:8).
   Your success is guaranteed by the Blood of Christ. Jesus hung on the cross being made a curse for you that you might be redeemed from the curse of poverty, sickness and spiritual death. You are now blessed with the blessing of Abraham (Galatians 3:13-14). God is your source and provider. The Lord sees your need, sees the supply and sees to it that your need is met, according to His riches in glory by Christ Jesus (Philippians 4:19).

5. **Jehovah-Rohi – The Lord your shepherd** (Psalm 23; John 10:10-11).
   Jesus, the good Shepherd came to earth and laid down His life for you so that you may have and enjoy life, and have it in abundance, to the full, till it overflows (John 10:10). The Lord is your Shepherd and you shall not want (Psalm 23:1). Delight yourself in the Lord and He will give you the desires of your heart (Psalm 37:4). No good thing will He withhold from you as you walk uprightly, trusting, obeying and reverencing Him (Psalm 84:11).

Make a study of the many other names of God and Jesus; some of Their names are: the Apostle and High Priest, the Lifter of your head, the Bread of Life, the God of Hope (Romans 15:13), the Horn of Salvation (faithful and true), the Wisdom of God, the Strength of your Life (Psalms 27:1); the Lord of Glory (1 Corinthians 2:8). There are numerous other names of God that reveal many dimensions of His kindness toward you (Psalm 9:10).

Step 2:

"Your kingdom Come..."

Consecrate yourself to the Lordship of Jesus Christ and His Word. Declare that His will will dominate your life today. Ask God for His promises to be established in your life today (Philippians 1:10).

Step 3:

"Your will be done on earth as it is in Heaven..."

Pray, declare, decree and bind the enemy regarding the will of God being done in your life, your family, your pastor your church, etc (Matthew 18:18; Proverbs 18:20; Psalm 45:1; Isaiah 54:17; Ephesians 6:10-18).

Step 4:

"Give us this day our daily bread..."

Pray according to John 16:23, 24, Philippians 4:6, 19, and Mark 11:24 for the needs of yourself, your spouse, your family, your friends, your church, your governmental leaders, etc. Remember to be continually filled with the Spirit

(Ephesians 5:18).
Step 5:

"Forgive us our debts as we forgive our debtors..."

Let the Spirit of God search your heart, wait patiently for Him. If there is sin, confess it and forsake it (Psalm 139:23, 24; Proverbs 28:13; 1 John 1:7-9). Pray over your heart that you would be able to forgive, abound in love toward others (Ephesians 4:32), maintain a conscience void of offense before God and man (Acts 24:16), and that you would be established in the fear of the Lord and walk worthy of the Lord all day long (Proverbs 23:17; Colossians 1:10). Commit today to guard your heart diligently (Proverbs 4:23), and don't let unbelief come out of your mouth (Colossians 4:6).

Step 6:

"Lead us not into temptation..."

Make a decision to walk in the spirit, in the reality of who you truly are in Christ. Be true to the real you; pursue love, righteousness and truth. Flee from sin. Yield to the Holy Spirit and let Him direct your paths. "Where the Spirit has Lordship there is liberty" (2 Corinthians 3:17). *"Walk in the Spirit and you will not fulfill the lust of the flesh"* (Galatians 5:16).

Step 7:

"Deliver us from evil..."

    1. Put on the whole armor of God.

2. Plead the Blood of Christ on yourself, your mind, your family and others.

3. Declare there is a wall of protection around you that the enemy cannot cross (John 1:10; Isaiah 33:21). Study these 'surround' scriptures and declare the Lord's protection and deliverance surrounds you. I suggest you write them down and read them every day until they are embedded in your heart.

Psalm 3:3	The Lord is a shield around you.
Isaiah 33:21	The Lord is as a wide river of protection between you and the enemy.
Zechariah 2:5	The Lord is a wall of fire around you.
Psalm 125:2	The Lord is a mountain around you.
Psalm 32:7	You are surrounded by songs of deliverance.
Psalm 32:10	Mercy surrounds you.
Psalm 34:7	The angels of the Lord surround you.
Psalm 5:12	The favour of the Lord surrounds you.

4. Declare that Psalm 91 belongs to you because you know God's name (Psalm 91:14), because you have set your love upon Him (Psalm 91:14), because you have made the Lord your dwelling place (Psalm 91:9), and because you have what you believe in your heart and say with your mouth (Mark 11:23).

5. Believe, say, declare and decree right now: "I dwell in the secret place of the Most High and abide under the shadow of the Almighty." I say, "the Lord is my refuge and fortress. No evil shall befall me. Amen" (Psalm 91:1, 2, 10).

You are living in an evil time. You need to build a wall of protection around your life and family so that you will not fear. Continue to believe that no terror will come near you and no weapon formed against you will prosper, because your righteousness, defense and authority is from the Lord (Isaiah 54:14, 17).

Step 8:

"For Yours is the kingdom and the power and the glory..."

Give God thanks and praise for hearing and answering your prayers. Acknowledge that His kingdom, His power, His anointing and His glory are within you right now (James 5:16; Luke 17: 21; Luke 12:32; Luke 10:19; Colossians 1:27; 2 Corinthians 1:21). Declare that the name of Jesus is above every name and that at the name of Jesus every knee shall bow and every tongue shall confess that Jesus Christ is Lord (Philippians 2:10, 11).

This prayer guide is an outline and a frame of reference. Be led by the Spirit of God. It is good to talk to men about God, but it is great to talk to God about men. May you be as a new, sharp, threshing instrument, in God's hand (Isaiah 41:15).

Spiritual Insight and Maturity

Blessed be God my Father, and Father of my Lord Jesus Christ, Who has blessed me with every spiritual blessing in the heavenly places in Christ (Ephesians 1:3). I pray Father, God of my Lord Jesus Christ, the Father of glory, that you give to me the spirit of wisdom and revelation in the knowledge of You, that the eyes of my understanding be enlightened; that I may know what is the hope of Your calling, what are the riches of the glory of Your inheritance in me, and what is the exceeding greatness of Your power toward me who believe, according to the working of Your mighty power which You worked in Christ when You raised Him from the dead and seated Him at Your right hand in the heavenly, far above all principality, power, might and dominion, and every name that is named, not only in this age but also in that which is to come. And You put all under His feet, and gave Him to be head over all to the church, which is His body, the fullness of Him who fills all in all (Ephesians 1:17-23).

I bow my knees to you Father. and pray that You would grant me, according to the riches of Your glory, to be strengthened with might through Your Spirit in my inner man, that Christ may dwell in my heart through faith, that I, being rooted and grounded in You, God may be able to comprehend with all the saints what is the width and length and depth and height and to know the love of Christ which passes knowledge; that I may be filled with all the fullness of God (Ephesians 3:14-19).

I pray that my love may abound still more and more in knowledge and all discernment, that I may approve the things that are excellent, that I may be sincere and without offense until the day of Christ, being filled with the fruits of righteousness which are by Jesus Christ, to the glory and praise of God (Philippians 1:9-11). I pray Father and ask that I be filled with the knowledge of Your will in all wisdom and spiritual understanding, that I may walk worthy of You Lord, fully pleasing You, being fruitful in every good work and increasing in the knowledge of God, strengthened with all might, according to Your glorious power, for all patience and longsuffering with joy, giving thanks to You Father who has qualified me to be partaker of the inheritance of the saints in the light, and has delivered me from the power of darkness and conveyed me into the kingdom of the Son of Your love, in whom I have redemption through His blood, the forgiveness of sins (Colossians 1:9-14).

Help me Lord to continue earnestly in prayer, being vigilant in it with thanksgiving. I pray also that You, Father God would open to me a door for the Word, to speak the mystery of Christ, that I may make it manifest as I ought to speak. Help me walk in wisdom toward those who are outside, redeeming the time. Let my speech always be with grace, seasoned with salt, that I may know how I ought to answer each one (Colossians 4:2-6). Father God, I pray that I may stand perfect and complete in Your will (Colossians 4:12b), and that I may be approved by You to be entrusted with the Gospel, not as pleasing men, but pleasing God who tests my heart (1 Thessalonians 2:4). Cleanse me from secret faults. Keep me back from presumptuous sins; let them not have dominion over me. Then I shall be blameless and I shall be innocent of great transgression. Let the words of my mouth and the meditation of my heart be acceptable in Your sight, O Lord, my strength and my redeemer (Psalm 19:12-14).

Lord God, make me increase and abound in love to all so that You may establish my heart blameless in holiness before You at the coming of my Lord Jesus Christ with all saints (1 Thessalonians 3:12-13). Sanctify me completely and may my whole spirit, soul and body be preserved blameless at the coming of my Lord Jesus Christ. God who called me is faithful, who also will do it (1 Thessalonians 5:23-24). Now may the God of peace who brought up our Lord Jesus from the dead, that great Shepherd of the sheep, through the Blood of the everlasting covenant, make me complete in every good work to do His will, working in me what is well pleasing in His sight, through Jesus Christ, to whom be glory forever and ever. Amen (Hebrews 13:20-21).

Father, let the sharing of my faith become effective by the acknowledgment of every good thing which is in me in Christ Jesus (Philemon 6). Thank you, Lord God, that grace and peace is multiplied to me in the knowledge of You and of Jesus my Lord, as Your divine power, has given to me all things that pertain to life and godliness, through the knowledge of You who called me by glory and virtue, by which have been given to me exceedingly great and precious promises, that through these I may be partaker of the divine nature, having escaped the corruption in the world through lust. Father, help me to be diligent, to add to my faith virtue, to virtue knowledge, to knowledge self-control, to self-control perseverance, to perseverance godliness, to godliness brotherly kindness, and to brotherly kindness love. Because these are mine and abound, I will be neither barren nor unfruitful in the knowledge of my Lord Jesus Christ, and I will never stumble, and an entrance will be supplied to me abundantly into the everlasting kingdom of my Lord and Saviour Jesus Christ (2 Peter 1:2-11).

In the name of Jesus Christ my Lord and Saviour, Amen! And all glory, majesty, praise, honor, power, dominion, and thanks be unto You Lord God, Hallelujah!

Also see: Psalm 23; Psalm 91; Psalm 103; Isaiah 54:8-17

Discerning the Blood of Christ

Precious Father, I thank You for delivering my life from the devil's authority and dominion, and giving me redemption through the Blood of Christ, even the forgiveness of my sins (Colossians 1:13,14). Jesus is my propitiation and I am made Your very own righteousness in Christ (Romans 3:25). My conscience is purged from every sense of guilt and inferiority (Hebrews 9:14). I have peace, reconciliation and favour with You (Colossians 1:20). I have access with confidence into Your very presence by the Blood of Jesus (Hebrews 10:19). Christ has become a curse for me and broke the power of sin, sickness and poverty off my life (Galatians 3:13). Jesus' blood continues to cleanse me as I walk in the light and in Your love (1 John 1:7).

There is resurrection power in the Blood. You raised up Jesus from the dead through the Blood of the everlasting covenant (Hebrews 13:20), as You saw the travail of His soul and Your divine justice was satisfied (Isaiah 53:11). You sent forth Your light and truth (Psalm 43:3) into the bowels of hell and raised Christ from the dead by Your glory (Romans 6:4), declaring "You are my Son, this day I have begotten You. And again I will be to You a Father and You shall be to me a Son" (Hebrews 1:5). You raised Jesus from the dead by the might of Your Spirit (Romans 8:11). Oh, that I may know Him and the power of His resurrection, the exceeding greatness of that power that was demonstrated when You raised Jesus from the dead. May I know the fellowship of His suffering, and be made conformable unto His death (Philippians 3:10; Ephesians 1:1-20).

As the blood of Abel cried out from the earth (Genesis 4:10) for justice and truth, even so the sanctifying Blood of Christ (Hebrews 13:12), by which I have been sprinkled (Hebrews 11:28; 1 Peter 1:2), speaks from the mercy seat of God

(Hebrews 12:24). The voice and testimony of the Blood (1 John 5:8,9) declares my victory, protection, deliverance and wholeness. I am covered with the Blood. There is perfecting power in the Blood. Father I pray in Jesus' Name that the Blood of the everlasting covenant would make me perfect in every good work to do Your will (Hebrews 13:20-21). May I be made perfect in obedience (1 Peter 1:2), loving not my life even unto death (Revelation 12:11). Let my ears, heart and will always hear the cries of Jesus' Blood, demanding my all, my whole-hearted consecration and my devotion to Your will, dear Father.

Help me, Father, to walk in love and unity with all believers as I discern the Body of Christ and honour the Blood (1 Corinthians 11:29), that makes us one in Him (Ephesians 2:13-14). Jesus came not to just redeem me from sin, but to redeem me to You, O Father (Revelation 5:9), and to bring many sons to glory (Hebrews 2:10). I receive grace to reckon the old man dead (Romans 6:11). I have been crucified with Christ—I have no self will. Help me to walk in communion with the Blood (I Corinthians 10:16) in the new and living way that Jesus has consecrated for us, the way of the Blood (Hebrews 10:20). The blood makes way for the glory.

Spiritual Momentum

Father, in the name of Jesus, I pray for spiritual momentum that I may grow, move on, be established and excel in the things of God, the things of the Kingdom of God and the will of God. Grant me your mercy and grace in abundance that I would resist sin, procrastination, slothfulness, passivity, and legalism. Deliver me from temptation, evil, and persecution. Strengthen me with might by your Spirit in my spirit. Let Your Word dwell in me richly. Grant that I would walk in fellowship and communion with the Blood of Jesus and be an overcomer by the word of my testimony. Let no weapon formed against me prosper. Grant me a broken and a contrite heart, a spirit of repentance, a spirit of prayer and intercession and a lifestyle of fasting. Grant me a spirit of strong courage, giving no place to the devil or fear and a heart that would cleave unto You. Empower me that I might live, speak and walk boldly before God and man. Empower me to walk in my authority as a believer, son and servant of the Most High God. Let signs and wonders, deliverance and healing, gifts and manifestations of Your Spirit be demonstrated through the name of Your Holy Son, Jesus. Amen.

Consecration

I pray Father in the name of Jesus, and I declare that I am willing and obedient to my Lord Jesus Christ, to His word and to the voice of His Spirit. I am determined to be continually fed and led by Your Word, continually sanctified by Your Spirit and continually cleansed by the Blood of Jesus. I put away all evil and wrong doing. Teach me to do what is right, to seek and do justice, to encourage the oppressed, to defend the cause of the fatherless, to plead the case of the widows and to have pity on the poor. Teach me, Lord, to hate evil and love good. Let me be rich in good works. Dear Father, fill me with Your love for You, for my family, for my neighbors and for my enemies. Place Your desires and passions in my heart, in my mind and in my soul. Cause me to walk in Your ways and fulfill Your purposes and desires of Your heart. Give me a spirit full of Your compassion, Your love, Your peace, Your joy, Your hope, Your gentleness, Your patience, Your longsuffering, Your goodness, Your kindness, Your discipline, Your self-control, Your faithfulness, Your meekness, Your godliness, Your courage, Your diligence, Your watchfulness, Your vigilance, Your wisdom and Your fullness. Let me be consumed by You, Lord God. Jesus, in my life be all in all to me and through me. Let Your will be done in my life. Perfect everything concerning me for Your glory.

Repentance

Have mercy on me, O God. According to Your loving-kindness blot out my transgressions, wash me thoroughly from mine iniquity (Psalm 51:1). Give me a repentant heart that is zealous for Your correction and quick to repent (Revelation 3:19).

Forgive me Lord for not giving You and Your Word first place in my life (Revelation 2:4). Forgive me for being lukewarm (Revelation 3:16), and for harbouring resentment, bitterness, and unforgiveness in my heart. Forgive me for not seeking Your face daily. Forgive me for taking Your presence and fellowship lightly (Leviticus 19:30). Forgive me for not trusting You enough, and for giving place to the devil through an evil heart of unbelief (Hebrews 3:12).

In the Name of Jesus, I put away all these besetting sins (Hebrews 12:1), and I return to You with my whole heart (Jeremiah 24:7). O Lord, create in me a clean heart and a steadfast, unwavering attitude of mind (Psalm 51:10). Your glory comes only to the broken and contrite spirit. To the one who trembles at Your Word (Isaiah 66:2), and knows that there is nothing good in himself (Romans 7:18). I am completely void of any personal ability in myself to do anything for You (John 15:5). I must have You in my life. I beseech You, O Lord to have complete control of my life. Fill me with Your Holy Spirit.

I receive the power of Your Spirit today to crucify the flesh and say, Yes, to You Lord. Yes, Lord! Here I am, send me

(Isaiah 6:8).

Sanctification

The overwhelming desire of my heart is that I may dwell in Your presence all the days of my life and behold Your beauty, O Lord. Teach me Your ways, and I will keep Your precepts with my whole heart.

I receive Your grace that I may walk worthy of You Lord, fully pleasing You, being fruitful in every good work and increasing in the knowledge of You Lord God.

I cry out, O Lord, for the refining fire of Your presence to purge, purify, and sanctify me wholly, that I may offer to You sacrifices that are well pleasing in Your sight. I am zealous for Your correction dear Master. Sanctify me in my spirit, soul, and body. In everything let the motives of my heart be pure. Let my tongue be a wholesome tree of life. Let my walk be upright and established in the way of holiness.

I worship You Lord for all of Your goodness. I will take heed to Your Word as to a light that shines in a dark place, until the day dawns and the day star rises in my heart. (Psalm 27:4; Psalm 119:68,69; Colossians 1:10; Malachi 3:3; Revelation 3:19; 1 Thessalonians 5: 23; Proverbs 15:4; Proverbs 16:17; 2 Peter 1:19).

A Perfect Heart

Father I come to You in the name of Jesus, and I pray concerning my heart, that it would be prepared and fixed in righteousness and true holiness. I pray concerning my heart, that it would be perfected in Christ. To whom is the arm of the Lord revealed? (Isaiah 53:1) To him that is of a poor and of a contrite spirit and trembles at Your Word (Isaiah 66:1). Grant me, O Lord, a broken heart and a contrite spirit, for You Lord are near to those who have a broken heart; and save such as have a contrite spirit (Psalm 34:18). Let my heart be pure that I may see You, O God (Matthew 5:8), and let me follow peace with all men and holiness, without which no man shall see You Lord (Hebrews 12:14).

Let me be a true worshipper, worshipping You Father in Spirit and in Truth; for You seek such to worship You (John 4:23). Oh that I would worship You Lord in the beauty of holiness (Psalm 29:2), giving to You Lord, the glory due to Your name (Psalm 29:2), coming before Your presence with thanksgiving and with singing (Psalm 100:2). In Your presence is fullness of joy, at Your right hand there are pleasures forevermore (Psalm 16:11). I will enter Your gates with thanksgiving and enter into Your courts with praise (Psalm 100:4), for You are holy, O You Who inhabits the praises of Israel (Psalm 21:3). The Lord my God looked down from heaven on the children of men, to see if there were any that did understand and seek God (Psalm 14: 2). Lord, help me understand and seek you.

Lord who shall abide in Your tabernacle? who shall dwell in Your holy hill (Psalm 15:1)? He that walks uprightly, and works righteousness, and speaks the truth in his heart (Psalm 15:2). How great is Your goodness which You have laid up for those who fear You (Psalm 31:19). Oh that I would fear You Lord, as Your saint, for there is no want to them that fear You (Psalm 34: 9). The secret of the Lord is with them that fear Him (Psalm 25:14). Teach me the fear of the Lord (Psalm 34:11): that I may keep my tongue from evil and my lips from speaking guile, that I may depart from evil and do good, and seek peace and pursue it (Psalm

34:13,14). Those who fear You, You shall hide them in the secret place of Your presence (Psalm 31:19-20). You shall keep them secretly in Your pavilion (Psalm 32:20). He who dwells in the secret place of the Most High shall abide under the shadow of the Almighty (Psalm 91:1).

Who shall stand in Your Holy place? Let my hands be clean and my heart pure that I may ascend to Your hill and stand in Your Holy place (Psalm 24:3,4). The eyes of the Lord run to and fro through the whole earth to show Himself strong on behalf of those whose heart is perfect towards Him (2 Chronicles 16:9). Lord, create in me a heart that is perfect (loyal) towards you. For You do not desire sacrifice, or else I would give it: You do not delight in burnt offering. Your sacrifices, O God, are a broken spirit: a broken and a contrite heart (Psalm 51:16,17). Oh that my offering to You O Lord, would be an offering in righteousness (Malachi 3:3). I will offer in Your tabernacles sacrifices of joy (Psalm 17: 6) and thanksgiving (Psalm 107:22). I will bring the sacrifices of praise to Your house O Lord (Jeremiah 33:11). I will render to You the calves of my lips (Hosea 14:2) . I will offer to you the sacrifices of praise continually, the fruit of my lips giving thanks and confessing Your name (Hebrews 13:15). I am a holy priesthood called to offer up spiritual sacrifices acceptable to You O Father by Jesus Christ (1 Peter 2:5). I will present my body a living sacrifice; holy and acceptable to You, O God, which is my reasonable service (Romans 12:2). For I am bought with a price and choose to glorify you in my body, my mind, and my heart, and my spirit which are Yours, O God (1 Corinthians 6:20).

To do good and to communicate I forget not, for with such sacrifices you are well pleased (Hebrews 13:10). Yet, I choose a more excellent way (1 Corinthians 12; 31): I choose love, I choose obedience which is better than sacrifices (1 Samuel 15: 22). I choose justice and judgement which is more acceptable to You, O Lord (Proverbs 21:3). I yield myself to obedience, to righteousness, to holiness (Romans 6:16,19). I pray O Lord for grace to perfect holiness in the fear of God (2 Corinthians 7:1), and that I be clothed with humility, for You O God resists the proud and gives grace to the humble (1 Peter 5:5).

I know also my God, that You test the heart; and have pleasure in uprightness (1 Chronicles 29:17). You have no greater joy than to hear that your children walk in truth (3 John 4), in love, in righteousness, and holiness, and that they be filled with all Your fullness, O God (Ephesians 3:19), and that they are walking worthy of You, well pleasing to You (Colossians 1:10). Oh that I would be as the apple of Your eye, and that I would hide under Your shadow (Psalm 17:8). Let my prayers be set forth before You as incense and the lifting up of my hands as the evening sacrifices (Psalm 141:2). In Jesus' Name I pray. Amen.

The Fear of The Lord

Teach me O Lord to number my days, that I may apply my heart unto wisdom (Psalm 90:12). Your fear Lord is wisdom (Job 28:28). I desire to dwell in Your fear Lord all the day long (Proverbs 23:17). Give me a broken spirit, a broken and a contrite heart which You will not despise, O God (Psalm 51:17). Put Your fear in my heart, O Lord, that I might not depart from You (Jeremiah 32:40).

Let me have grace that I may serve You, O Lord, with reverence and godly fear. For You, O God, are a consuming fire (Hebrews 12:28-29). Teach me to walk circumspectly not as a fool but as wise, redeeming and discerning the time (Ephesians 5:15-16). The night is far spent, the day is at hand (Romans 13:12). Behold, the day is coming burning like an oven. The great and dreadful day of the Lord; all who do wickedly shall be stubble. And the day which is coming shall burn them up, says the Lord of Host (Malachi 4:1, 5).

I choose the fear of the Lord (Proverbs 1:29). I choose to tremble at Your Word (Isaiah 66:2). I am determined to be found faithful to You, O Lord, watching and waiting with my vessel full of oil at Your coming (Matthew 25:21,13,4). Teach me Your way O Lord, I will walk in Your truth. Unite my heart to fear Your name (Psalm 86:11).

I will work out my salvation with fear and trembling (Philippians 2:12). I will keep my tongue from evil, and my lips from speaking guile. I will depart from evil and do good. I will seek peace and pursue it (Psalm 34:13,14). I will be zealous for the correction of the Lord (Revelation 3:19), that I might be perfected in holiness (2 Corinthians 7:1, Hebrews 12:10), and that I may dwell in Your presence Lord forever. This is the heritage of those that fear Your name (Psalm 61: 5,7).

Open Doors

Father, in the Name of Jesus, I confess and declare that according to Your Word, you are loosing the loins of kings and opening before me the two leaved gates. You are going before me, and making the crooked places straight. You are breaking in pieces the gates of brass and cutting asunder the bars of iron (Isaiah 45:1,2). You are opening doors and no man shall shut them (Revelation 3:8).

The gifts and the anointing are making a way for me even where there seems to be no way (Proverbs 18: 16). The kings heart is in the hand of the Lord, as rivers of water You turn it whither so ever You will (Proverbs 21:1). When a man's way pleases the Lord, He will make even his enemies to be at peace with him (Proverbs 16:7). No weapon formed against me shall prosper, and every tongue that rises against me in judgement I shall condemn. This is my heritage as a servant of the Lord (Isaiah 54:17). You are surrounding me with favour as with a shield (Psalm 5:12). God is bringing me into favour and tender love with the princes, kings, and those in authority. Promotion comes from God (Daniel 1:9; Psalm 75:6).

My Father is opening to me doors of utterance, to speak the mystery of Christ (Colossians 4:3). He is giving me utterance that I may open my mouth boldly to make known the mystery of the gospel (Ephesians 6:19). God is giving me knowledge and skill in learning, and wisdom, and understanding in the mystery of God and all visions and dreams (Daniel 1:17; Colossians 2:2).

Thank you Father in Jesus' name. Amen.

The Unsaved

Father, I ask You in the name of Jesus for the salvation of _____. I know that it is not Your will that _____ should perish, but rather it is Your will that (he/she) should come to repentance (2 Peter 3:9) and the knowledge of the Truth (1 Timothy 2:4).

I thank You Father that in Christ You have reconciled _____ to Yourself. You are not holding his/her sins against him/her (2 Corinthians 5:19). Jesus paid the price in full through His shed blood (Romans 3:25) for _____ to be set free from sin and the devil's dominion (Romans 6:14). Jesus has fulfilled every righteous requirement of the law on _____'s behalf (Romans 8:4). Therefore, the handwriting of the requirements that were against _____ has been effectively wiped out (Colossians 2:14) by Jesus' sacrifice as the Lamb of God (John 1:29).

Satan, the god of this world has blinded _____'s mind and kept him/her in unbelief and darkness 2 Cor.4:4). But in the name of Jesus, I now break the power of the devil over _____'s life. In the name of Jesus I bind every blinding spirit and influence off _____'s mind (Matthew 16:19). In the name of Jesus, with the truth of God's living Word, I cast down and demolish every theory, philosophy, reasoning, belief system, or other barrier that is deceptive, erroneous, and exalts itself against the knowledge of God, and I bring into captivity every thought to the obedience of Christ (2 Corinthians 10:5).

Through the redemptive power of the Blood of Christ I declare and decree release and deliverance for _____ from the devil's hold and authority in Jesus' Name (Colossians 1:13-14; Zechariah 9:11).

Father, I pray that You will send the right labourers to _____ to share and minister to him/her the gospel of Christ (Matthew 9:38). The gospel is the power of God unto salvation for _____ (Romans 1:16)

I pray, Lord, that You would open his/her spiritual ears and eyes, and cause him/her to hear and see what the Spirit of the Lord is speaking to him/her (Ephesians 1:17-18). Draw him/her by Your Spirit O Lord (John 6:44) to Yourself. Convict him/her of sin, of righteousness, and of judgement

(John 16:8-11).

Father, I ask that You would use miracles, signs, wonders, dreams, visions, or any other means possible to bring _____ to Yourself (Romans 15:18-19; Acts 19:11-18).

By faith I call _____ saved and delivered from the enemy's influence and kingdom (Romans 4:17; Colossians 1:13). I say this is the day of salvation for _____ (2 Corinthians 6:2).

Jesus, You are a wonderful Saviour. Thank You Lord for saving _____.

Prayer Keys from James 5:16

James 5:16 says, *"Confess your faults one to another and pray one for another that you may be healed."* The amplified Bible adds, *"the earnest heart-felt continued prayer of a righteous man makes tremendous power available, dynamic in its working. "*

Here are five keys from James 5:16 to make your prayers powerful and dynamic:

1. Confess your faults one to another. Do not allow offenses in your heart.

2. Pray one for another. The Lord turned the captivity of Job when he prayed for his friends (Job 42:10)

3. Effectual prayer. Pray the Word; what we ask according to His will (His Word He hears us, and our petitions are granted I John 5:14,15).

4. Be fervent - let your prayers he earnest, heartfelt

and passionate.

5. You are righteous in Christ - live clean, and do not allow condemnation (Romans 8:1; 1 John 3:11).

Based on: James 5:16; John 6:63; 2 Corinthians 10:4; 1 Peter 3:12

The words that I speak in prayer, they are the Words of God. They are Spirit and Life, and mighty through God to pull down strongholds. God's eyes are over the righteous, and His ears are open to my cry. God hears my prayers. My prayers avail much. They bring salvation to the sinner, deliverance to the oppressed, healing to the sick, and prosperity to the poor. My prayers will usher in the next move of God in my church, my city and in the earth. Praise the Lord.

Section III: *Prayer*

B. Prayers for Pastors

"Pray for me, that utterance may be given to me, that I may open my mouth boldly to make known the mystery of the gospel"
(Ephesians 6:19).

Pastor's Prayer

Father, in the name of Jesus I pray and confess that the Spirit of the Lord rests upon me. You have anointed me and made me able to teach and minister Your Word. I am totally reliant on the Holy Spirit for He enables me to perform my task. I have the Spirit of wisdom and understanding, the Spirit of counsel and might, the Spirit of knowledge and the fear of the Lord. My delight is in the fear of the Lord. I am filled with the knowledge of God's will in all wisdom and spiritual understanding. The Spirit of truth guides me into all truth, and teaches me to rightly divide the word of truth. The Spirit of truth brings all things to my remembrance as I have need of them. The Holy Spirit teaches me what I ought to say so that I am able to present the Word of God accurately, simply, and in a practical manner, and with power.

Father, grant unto me your servant that I may open my mouth boldly and declare Your Word. Grant O Lord, that doors of utterance would be open to me to bear witness to the Word of Your grace. Grant that signs and wonders may be done by my hands through the name of Your Holy servant, Jesus. I thank you that I am righteous, and that I am as bold as a lion. I am a believer and signs accompany me. I have received power because the Holy Spirit has come upon me and He indwells me. I have faith in the name of Jesus Christ of Nazareth, whom God raised from the dead. In the name of Jesus, I drive out devils, and I speak with new tongues; when I lay hands on the sick they recover.

Father, I thank you for the Spirit of love, power, and self control. I am diligent and I study to show myself approved unto God. I am persistent in prayer. I am an example of the believers in word, in manner of life, in love, in spirit, in faith, and in purity. I follow after righteousness, godliness, faith, love, patience, and meekness. I am not ashamed of the gospel for it is the power of God unto salvation to all them that believe. God is my confidence and my strength. In Him I trust.

Lord as I preach and teach, let me not speak by the will of man nor mine own will, But let me be moved, influenced, and carried away by the Holy Spirit. Let me speak the words and oracles of God in Jesus' name and might. (Luke 4:18; 1 Timothy 1:12; 1 John 2:20; Isaiah 11:2; Ephesians 1: 17; II Timothy 2: 7; Colossians 1: 9; John 16:13; 2 Timothy 2: 15; John 14:26; Luke 12: 12; Acts 4:29; Ephesians 6: 19; Acts 14:3; Acts 4:30; Proverbs 28:1; Mark 16:17; Acts 1:8; Acts 4:10; 2 Timothy 1:7; Romans 12:11; 2 Timothy 2:15; Romans 12:12; 1 Timothy 4:12; 1 Timothy 6:11; Romans 1:16; 2 Corinthians .3:5).

Prayer for your Church

Father God, we pray and believe today that _____ (place your church's name here) will be all that You intend for us to be. Through Your grace and sufficiency may we accomplish the dreams and desires of your heart for us.

Help us O Lord, to be Your instrument that would bring salvation and wholeness to the individual, his family, and his relationships. Help us to effectively represent Your heart and be a sweet fragrance of Christ to our community, to our city of (your city), to our country of (your country), and to the world.

Lord I ask in faith that Your anointing and grace be multiplied upon our pastor, our leaders, and each of us.

Grant us the Spirit of wisdom and understanding, the Spirit of counsel and of might, the Spirit of knowledge and the fear of the Lord (Isaiah 11:2).

Help us to walk in obedience, humility, integrity, and truth. Teach us to be kind, loving, and warm towards each other. Pour out a Spirit of prayer upon us and help us to be faithful and strong in faith. Give us a Spirit of unity and love.

When the day is done and it is time to receive our rewards and crowns, may we hear You say, _____ (your church) was faithful over a few things, so I made them rulers over many things (Matthew 25:21). Though their beginning was small, their latter end was greatly increased (Job 8:7).

Lord, perfect everything concerning us (Psalm 138:8).

What to Pray for your Pastors & Leaders

Your leaders need your prayers: Romans 15:30; Ephesians 6:18-20; Philippians 1:19; Heb.13:18.

Six Main Things to always Pray for (Proverbs 22:4; Acts 6:4):

    1. The fear of God
    2. Humility
    3. Hunger for God
    4. Holiness
    5. Love of the Word
    6. Desire to Pray

Pray that they would understand their calling and their

responsibilities:

1. Feed the flock of God (I Peter 5:2).

2. Declare & teach the full counsel of God (Acts 20:27,28).

3. Equip and perfect the saints (Ephesians 4:11-13).

4. Teach & make disciples of Christ (Matthew 28:19).

5. Teach, preach, exhort, instruct, & correct (2 Timothy 4:2; 2 Timothy 3:16-17; Revelation 3:19; 2 Timothy 2:24-26; Hebrews 12:10; 1 Thessalonians 3:10).

6. Comfort and support the sheep (1 Thessalonians 5:14).

7. Warn the sheep (1 Thessalonians 5:14; Colossians 1:28).

8. Turn the people to righteousness (Daniel 12:3).

9. Turn the people away from iniquity & sin (Malachi 2:6).

10. Turn the peoples heart to God (Malachi 4:6).

11. Pray they would be found faithful stewards of God (1 Corinthians 4:2).

12. They would serve with fear & trembling (1 Corinthians 3:8-15; 1Corinthians 2:3; Hebrews 13:17).

13. They would be diligent in fulfilling their call (2 Peter 1:10).

14. They would earnestly contend for the faith (Jude 3).

15. They would think, speak, and conduct themselves as an

ambassadors of Christ (2 Corinthians 5:20).

16. For their total surrender to God, (Acts 20:24; 2 Corinthians 4:10; John 12:24-26; Matthew 10:37-40; 2 Corinthians 4:17).

17. They would speak not their own words & mind, but speak as an oracle of God (1 Peter 4:11).

18. That the Word would abide in them richly (Colossians 3:16; Joshua 1:8; 2 Timothy 2:15; 1 Timothy 4:15; Proverbs 4:20-23; Deuternomy 30:14; Psalm 119:11; Jeremiah 15:16).

19. That the Word of God will fill their mouths (Isaiah 49:1; Isaiah 50:4; Isaiah 58:13; Psalm 45:1,2; Jeremiah 23:29; Jeremiah 15:19; Jeremiah 1:5; Jeremiah 5:14).

20. That they would have divine utterance, (Job 32:8; Proverbs .20:27; Psalm 18:28; Psalm 119:105; Psalm 119:130).

21. That the Spirit of prophecy will operate in their teaching & preaching (Revelation 19:10).

22. That they would have the mind of Christ (Philippians 2:5; 1 Corinthians 2:16).

23. That they would have the wisdom of God (1 Corinthians 1:30; Colossians 2:2,3; 1 John 2:20; 1 Corinthians 2:9-16).

24. Pray for them the following scriptures (Ephesians 1:16-23; Ephesians 3:16-20; Colossians 1:9-11; Isaiah 33:6).

25. That they would have clear vision (Habakkuk 2:2; Proverbs 29:17; Ecclesiastes 5:3).

26. To have God's priorities in their life (Matthew 6:33; Philippians 1:10; Phiippians 3:10-14).

27. To have a consistent & deep prayer life (Acts 6:4; Colossians 4:12; Romans 12:12).

28. To have intimate relationship with the Lord (Acts 9:31; Psalm 25:14; Psalm 4:3).

29. To be established in righteousness (Isaiah 54:14; Hebrews 5:14; Hebrews 10:2).

30. That the gifts of the Spirit, signs & wonders, special miracles will operate in their ministry (1 Corinthians 1:5,7; 1 Corinthians 12:31; Hebrews 2:4; Acts 19:11).

31. That they would be patient, meek, and gentle with all men (Galatians 6:1; 2 Timothy 2:24-25).

32. That they will seek only to please God always (Galatians 1:10; 1 Peter 4:1-2; 1 Thessalonians 2:4).

33. That they will never compromise truth (Proverbs 23:23; Romans 3:4; 3 John 3-4; 2 Corinthians 13:8).

34. That they will never compromise integrity (Psalm 15; Psalm 26:1; Psalm 25:21).

35. That they will always choose the Fear of the Lord and to honor God (Proverbs 1:29).

36. That they would understand and be established in the Fear of the Lord (Psalm 86:11; Jeremiah 32:40;

Proverbs 16:6; Proverbs 23:17).

37. That they would walk in purity (I Thessalonians 2:10).

38. That they would walk in holiness (Romans 1:4; 2 Corinthians 7:1; 2 Thessalonians 4:7; Psalm 93:5).

39. That they would maintain a pure conscience (Acts 24:16, 2 Corinthians 4:2).

40. To be pure in heart (Matthew 5:8).

41. To be of a broken & contrite heart (Psalm 51:17; Isaiah 66:2).

42. To have heart after God (Acts 13:22; 2 Chronicles 16:9)

43. That they would handle money with integrity and the Fear of the Lord (1 Peter 5:2,3).

44. That they would walk in meekness & humility (Proverbs 22:4; 1 Peter 5:5; Psalm 25:9; 2 Corinthians 10:1).

45. That they would be open to correction & godly counsel (Proverbs 1:23).

46. To have a zeal for correction (Revelation 3:19).

47. To love & care for the flock (1 Thessalonians 2:8; 1 Corinthians 14:1).

48. To walk & grow in love (1 Corinthians 13:4-8; Colossians 1:9).

49. To walk in the fruits of the Spirit (John 15:5; Galatians

5:22-23; 2 Peter 1:5-8).

50. To be rich in good works (Hebrews 10:24; Hebrews 6:10).

51. To walk in the Spirit (Galatians 5:16).

52. To be led by the Spirit (Romans 8:14).

53. To live in the Spirit (Galatians 5:25).

54. To be continually filled with the Spirit (Ephesians 5:18).

55. To be filled with joy, thanksgiving, & praises to God (Hebrews 13:15; Ephesians 5:19-20).

56. That they would give no place to the devil (Ephesians 4:27).

57. That they would not be ignorant of the devils tricks (2 Corinthians 2:11).

58. That they would make no provision for the flesh (Romans 13:14).

59. That they would buffet and mortify their flesh (1 Corinthians 9:27; Romans 8:13).

60. That they would live free from offense, bitterness, envy, strife, resentment, unforgiveness, ...etc. (2 Corinthians 2:11; Hebrews 12:15; Psalm 119:165; John 16:1; Proverbs 4:23; James 3:14-15).

61. Pray that every plot of the enemy against them will be brought to naught (1 Corinthians 2:6).

62. That no weapon formed against them will prosper (Isaiah 54:17).

63. That they would be kept in the presence of God free from the strife of tongues (Psalm 31:19).

64. Bind the powers of witchcraft and deception from touching their lives or families.

65. Plead the blood of Jesus upon them (Revelation 12:11).

66. Pray for their complete sanctification & wholeness (1 Thessalonians .5:23).

67. Pray for divine protection, (Psalm 91, Psalm 32:7).

68. Pray for angelic protection & ministry in their lives (Psalm 34:7; Hebrews 1:14; Psalm 103:20; Psalm 91:11).

69. That the mercy of God to surround them (Psalm 32:10)).

70. That the favor of God surround them (Psalm 5:12).

71. That grace would abound in their lives (2 Corinthians 9:8)

72. That they would walk in divine health (Romans 8:2; Romans 8:11; Proverbs 4:22).

73. Pray for agreement in their marriages (Amos 3:3)

74. Pray for their spouse & family (Psalm 128:3; Psalm 115:14)

75. For prosperity in every area of their life (Psalm 118:25; Psalm 35:27; Psalm 112:1-3; 3 John 2; Psalm 23:1; Psalm 34:9-10; Deuteronomy 28:1-14).

76. That the purpose of God to be fully accomplished, that the Lord would perfect and complete everything concerning them (Psalm 57:7; Psalm 138:8; Hebrews 13:20-21; Philippians. 2:13; 2 Thessalonians 2:11).

77. That the Lord would be glorified in their life (John 15:8; John 15:16; 1 Corinthians 1:34).

78. That in all things God might have preeminence (Colossians 1:18).

Note:

- Pray in faith (Heb. 11:6; Mark 11:24)
- Pray the Word (Eph. 6:17)
- Mix your prayer with thanksgiving, joy and tongues (Philippians 4:6; Philippians 1:4; 1 Corinthians 14:15).

You have authority in the Name of Jesus.

Whatsoever you bind or loosen on earth is bound or loosened in Heaven.

If two agree on earth as touching anything, it shall be done (Matt. 18:18-20).

Go to Church Expecting

King David said, *"I was glad when they said to me, let us go into the House of the Lord"* (Ps.122:1). Let us continue to assemble together in one accord, seek God's face, praise His Name, and feed on His Word. We will see the power and the glory of God in His House (Ps.63:2).Times of refreshing will come from the presence of the Lord (Acts 3:19). The Spirit of God will manifest among us in glorious ways. We are to hunger and thirst for the manifestation of the glory of God. They that hunger and thirst after righteousness shall be filled (Matt.5:6).

We are to come to church with expectation and anticipation of what The Lord will say and do among us. Paul said, he will see God's salvation and deliverance because of the prayers of his partners and because of his earnest expectation (Phil.1:19,20). The lame man at the temple gate in Acts 3:5 "looked on Peter and John expecting to receive something of them", and he was miraculously healed. Blind Bartimaeus threw away his beggar's coat in expectation of receiving his sight, and he was healed (Mark 10:50-52). So let us come to church every week hungry for God expecting Him to do great things. "Our expectation is from Him" Ps.62:5. King David said, "I was glad when they said to me, let us go into the House of the Lord" (Ps.122:1). Let us continue to assemble together in one accord, seek God's face, praise His Name, and feed on His Word. We will see the power and the glory of God in this House (Ps. 63:2).

Times of refreshing will come from the presence of the Lord (Acts 3:19). The Spirit of God will manifest among us in glorious ways. We are to hunger and thirst for the manifestation of the glory of God. They that hunger and thirst after righteousness shall be filled (Matt. 5:6).

Reminder: Speak the confessions and prayers out loud whenever possible. Faith comes by hearing and hearing the Word of God from your own lips.

Section IV

Biblical Meditations

"Meditate on these things; give yourself entirely to them, that your progress may be evident to all"
(1 Timothy 4:15).

Healing Scriptures

Meditate in God's Word daily (Joshua 1:8).

- I am the Lord Who heals you (Exodus 15:26). In other words, I am Jehovah your ROPHE – that is, your doctor, your physician, and your healer. God is One who repairs what He has made, not one who is inclined to abandon the work of His own hands.

- Bless the eternal Father, O my soul. Remember all His benefits: He pardons all your sins, and He heals all your sicknesses. (Psalm 103:2-3, MOFF).

- I am the Lord, I do not change (Malachi 3:6, TAY).

- I pray that you may in all respects prosper and enjoy good health, even as your soul prosper (3 Timothy 2, WEY-KJ).

- If you then, imperfect as you are, know enough to give your children what is good, how much more shall your Father, Who is in Heaven, give what is good to them that ask Him (Matthew 7:11).

- He did not spare His own Son, but gave Him up for us all, will He not with Him graciously give us everything else (Romans 8:32, WILLIAMS).

- Surely He has bore our grief (sicknesses, weaknesses, and distresses) and carried our sorrows and pains (of punishment), yet we (ignorantly) considered Him stricken, smitten, and afflicted by God (as of with leprosy). But He was wounded for our transgressions;

He was bruised for our guilt and iniquity. The chastisement needful to obtain peace and well being for us was upon Him, and with the stripes we are healed and made whole (Isaiah 53:4-5, AMP).

- I tell you then, when you ask for anything in prayer, you have only to believe that it is yours, and it will be granted you (Mark 11:24, KNOX).

- Is anyone sick among you? He should call in the elders of the church and they should pray over him, and anoint him with oil in the name of the Lord, and the prayer that is offered in faith will save the sick. The Lord will raise him to health, and if he has committed sins he will be forgiven. So practice confessing your sins to one another, and praying for one another, that you may be cured. An upright man's prayer, when it keeps at work, is very powerful (James 5:14-15, WILLIAMS).

- He sent His Word, and healed them, and delivered them from their destructions (Psalm 107:20, KJV).

- Do not be wise in your own eyes. Fear the Lord and shun evil. This will bring health to your body and nourishment to your bones (Proverbs 3:7-8, NIV).

- My son, attend to My Words, consent and subject to my sayings. Let them not depart from your sight. Keep them in the center of your heart. For they are life to those who find them, healing and health to all their flesh (Proverbs 4:20-22, AMP)

- A calm and undisturbed mind and heart are the life and health of the body. But envy, jealousy, and wrath are like rottenness to the bones (Proverbs 14:30, AMP).

* A cheerful heart is good medicine (Proverbs 17:22, ASV).

Prosperity Scriptures

OBEDIENCE:

If you will give ear to my Word and do it, the good things of the land will be yours (Isaiah 1:19, BAS).

Keep therefore the words of this covenant and do them, that you may prosper in all that you do (Deuteronomy 29:9, NKJ).

If they obey and serve Me, they shall spend their days in prosperity and their years in pleasure (Job 36:11, NKJ).

GIVING:

It is possible to give away and become richer! It is also possible to hold on too tightly and lose everything. Yes, the liberal man shall be rich! By watering others he waters himself (Proverbs 11:24-25, TAY).

Honour the Lord with your possessions and with the first fruits of all your increase. So your barns will be filled with plenty and your vats with new wine (Proverbs 3:9-10).

Give and it will be given to you, good measure, pressed down, shaken together, and running over will men give to your bosom. For with the same measure that you use, it shall be measured to you again (Luke 6:38).

PROSPERITY FACTS:

Blessed is the man who fears the Lord, who delights greatly in His commandments. His descendents will be mighty on earth. The generation of the upright will be blessed. Wealth and riches will be in his house (Psalm 112:1-3, NKJ).

The reward of humility and the fear of the Lord is riches, honour and life (Proverbs 22:4, RV).

You shall remember the Lord your God for it is He who gives you power to get wealth that He may establish His covenant (Deuteronomy 8:18, NKJ).

WEALTH TRANSFER:

"The silver is Mine, the gold is Mine" says the Lord of Hosts (Haggai 2:8, NKJ).

God gives wisdom and knowledge and joy to a man who is good in His sight, but to the sinner He gives the work of gathering and collecting that he may give to him who is good before God (Ecclesiastes 2:26, NKJ).

A good man leaves an inheritance to his children's children. But the wealth of the sinner is stored up for the righteous (Proverbs 13:22, NKJ).

This is the portion of a wicked man with God... though he heaps up silver like dust, and piles up clothing like clay, he may pile it up, but the just will wear it, and the innocent will divide the silver (Job 27:13,16,17, NKJ).

I will give you the treasures of darkness and hidden riches of secret places, that you may know that I the Lord, who call you by your name, am the God of Israel (covenant)

(Isaiah 45:3, NKJ).

PROMISES:

Thus says the Lord, your Redeemer, the Holy one of Israel: "I am the Lord your God who teaches you to profit, who leads you by the way you should go" (Is.48:17, NKJ).

My God shall supply all your need according to His riches in glory by Christ Jesus (Phil.4:19, NKJ).

Names for Believers

"Behold what manner of love the Father has bestowed on us, that we should be called children of God and therefore the world does not know us, because it did not know Him. Beloved, now we are children of God" (John 3:1,2).

1. Sons and Daughters — 2 Corinthians 6:18
2. Sons of God — Romans 8:14; Galatians 4:6
3. Heirs of God — Galatians 4:7; Romans 8:17
4. Joint heirs with Christ — Romans 8:17
5. Children of God — Galatians 3:26; Romans 8:16
6. Children of the promise — Colossians 4:28; Romans 9:8
7. Children of the free — Galatians 4:31
8. Children of the light — 1 Thess. 5:5, Ephesians 5:8
9. Children of the day — 1 Thessalonians 5:5
10. Light — 2 Corinthians 6:14
11. Righteousness — 2 Corinthians 6:14
12. Righteousness of God in Christ — 2 Corinthians 5:21
13. Temple of God — 2 Corinthians 6:16
14. God's Building — 1 Corinthians 3:9
15. God's Garden — 1 Corinthians 3:9

16. Partakers of His Promise	Ephesians 3:6
17. Fellow Heirs	Ephesians 3:6
18. Fellow Citizens with the Saints	Ephesians 2:19
19. The Household of God	Ephesians 2:19
20. The Family of God	Ephesians 3:15
21. The Elect of God	Colossians 3:12
22. Lively Stones	1 Peter 2:5
23. Holy Priesthood	1 Peter 2:5
24. Royal Priesthood	1 Peter 2:9
25. Holy Nation	1 Peter 2:9
26. Peculiar People	1 Peter 2:9
27. Kings	Revelation 1:6; Revelation 5:10
28. Priests	Revelation 1:6; Revelation 5:10
29. Branches	John 15:5
30. God in the Spirit	Philippians 3:3
31. Saints	1 Corinthians 1:2
32. Stewards of the Mysteries of God	1 Corinthians 4:1
33. Epistle of Christ	2 Corinthians 3:3
34. Ministries of Christ	1 Corinthians 4:1
35. Able Ministers of the New Testament	2 Corinthians 3:6
36. Ambassadors of Christ	2 Corinthians 5:20
37. Christ's	1 Corinthians 3:23
38. Sweet Savour of Christ	2 Corinthians 2:15
39. A New Creation	2 Corinthians 5:17
40. A New Man	Colossians 3:10; Ephesians 4:24
41. More than Conquerors	Romans 8:37

Don't believe the devil's lies, he is the accuser of the brethren (Revelation 12:10). Be true to the real you; walk worthy of the Lord. You are God's treasure. Think, talk and act in harmony with who you truly are.

Miscellaneous Scriptures

Righteousness:
Philippians 3:9; Isaiah 54:14; Isaiah 54:17; 1 John 4:17, 18; Hebrews 1:8

Kingdom of God:
Matthew 6:33; Romans 14:17; Luke 17:21; Luke 12:32; Psalms 103:19; Hebrews 1:8

Holiness:
2 Corinthians 7:1; Romans 1:4; Romans 6:19; 1 Thessalonians 4:17; 1 Peter 1:15, 16; Psalms 93:5

Love:
1 Corinthians 13:8; 1 Corinthians 13:4-8; I John 4:18; Matthew 22:37, 39; Deuteronomy 6:5; 1 John 2:5; John 17: 23, 26; 1 John 4:12

Wisdom:
1 Corinthians 1:30; Colossians 2:2,3; James 1:5; Proverbs 24:3; Proverbs 4:7; Proverbs 9:10

Fear of the Lord:
Proverbs 8:13; Psalm 25:14; Psalm 34:9-14; Malachi 1:6; Malachi 2:5; Malachi 4:2; Hebrews 12:28; Hebrews 4:1; Philippians 2:12; 2 Corinthians 7:1

Authority:
Luke 10:19; Matthew 28:20; Matthew 18:18; Romans 10:6; John 14:12-24

The Name of Jesus:
Philippians 2:9-11; Ephesians 1:19-27; Matthew 18:18-20; Mark 16:17, 18; Colossians 3:17

Deliverance:
Galatians 5:16; Romans 6:11; Galatians 5:24; Proverbs 18:21; Job 22:28; Proverbs 12:6

Glory:
Isaiah 35:2; Exodus 33:18,19; 2 Peter 1:4; Colossians 1:27; 2 Corinthians 3:18; Romans 6:4; John 11:40

Faith:
Romans 10:17; Hebrews 11:1; 2 Corinthians 5:7; Philemon 6; Romans 12:3; 2 Corinthians 4:13; Mark 11:23; 1 John 5:4; Galatians 5:6

Patience:
James 1:2, 3; Hebrews 6:12; Hebrews 10:35-39

Joy:
Isaiah 12:3; James 1:3; Romans 15:13; Psalm 126:5

Trust:
Proverbs 3:3-5; Psalm 62:8; Isaiah 26:3

Peace:
Isaiah 26:3; Philippians 4:6,7

Thoughts:
Philippians 4:8; Matthew 6:31; 2 Corinthians 10:4,5; Matthew 15:19; Psalm 119:11; Colossians 3:16

Mouth:
Proverbs 18:21; James 3:2; Colossians 4:6; Ephesians 4:29; Job 22:38; Proverbs 13:3; Psalm 141:1; Psalm 39:1

Truth:
John 8:31, 32; John 1:17; John 17:7; 2 Corinthians 13:8; Ephesians 6:14; 3 John 3,4; Proverbs 23:23; 2 Corinthians 13:8

Victory:
Romans 8:37; 1 John 5:4; 1 Corinthians 15:57; Revelations 12:11; Matthew 12:11

Reminder: Speak the confessions and prayers out loud whenever possible. Faith comes by hearing and hearing the Word of God from your own lips.

Section V

Conclusion

"Let us hear the conclusion of the whole matter: Fear God and keep His commandments, For this is the whole duty of man" (Ecclesiastes 12:13).

Food For Thought

1. I can't lie speaking the truth. The Word is truth.

2. Faith says what God says (Romans 3:3,4).

3. Faith speaks the truth.

4. Faith calls those things that be not as though they were (Romans 4:17).

5. According as it is written, I believe and therefore I speak (2 Corinthians 4:13).

6. I walk by faith an not by sight (2 Corinthian 5:7).

7. I am able to quench all the fiery darts of the wicked with the shield of faith (Ephesians 6:16).

8. According to my faith be it unto me (Matthew 9:29).

9. My confessions will affect my believing. My tongue is the pen of a ready writer (Psalms 45:1), writing on the tablet of my heart (Proverbs 3:3).

10. I hold fast to my confession (Hebrews 4:14).

11. I fight the good fight of faith (1 Timothy 6:12).

12. I earnestly contend for the faith (Jude 3).

13. My confession is my profession.

14. I can have what I say (Mark 11:23).

15. My words have authority (Proverbs 18:21).

16. Death and life are in the power of my tongue (Proverbs 18:21).

17. I confess right and I will have good success (Joshua 1:8).

18. I speak to the mountains (Mark 11:23).

19. I confess the Word.

20. I speak with a spirit of authority (2 Corinthians 4:13).

21. By my words I shall be justified or condemned (Matthew 12:37).

22. I am quick to hear and slow to speak (James 1:19).

23. I study to answer (Proverbs 15:28).

24. I let my heart instruct my mouth. (Proverbs 16:23).

25. I let the words of my mouth be accepted in God's sight (Psalm 19:14).

26. I let truth come out of my lips (Ephesians 4:15).

27. Lies are an abomination to my lips (Proverbs 8:7).

28. Jesus continually confessed His son-ship and mission. I do likewise.

29. I understand a wrong confession cancels my prayers and faith (Psalm 141:2,3).

30. My faith will not rise above my confession (Galatians 3:5)

31. I dare to say what God says about me, my circumstances, m family and others and I will become God's mouth piece in the earth.

32. My weapon is the sword of the Spirit which is the Word of God praying and speaking always (Ephesians 6:17, 18).

33. I let God be true and every man a liar so that I may be declared right (Romans 3:4)

34. The Word of God is not theory or speculation but rather certainty and truth (Proverbs 22:21).

35. My faith does not stand in the wisdom of men, i.e reasoning, sense, knowledge, etc., but rather in the power of God's Word (1 Corinthians 2:5).

36. The Word of God is the power of God unto salvation (Romans 1:16).

37. All things are upheld by the word of God's power (Hebrews 1:3).

38. No word of God is void of power or can go by default (Luke 1:37).

39. Forever the Word is settled in Heaven (Psalm 119:89).

Section V – Conclusion

40. When I know who I am in Christ and walk as I am in Christ, all hell will fear me.

41. The communication of my faith becomes effective when I acknowledge or own up to everything that is in me in Christ (Philemon 6).

42. If I do not walk in love my faith and prayers will be hindered (Galatians 5:6).

43. Prayer is an open door for the Holy Spirit to be involved in my life.

44. I am master because Jesus is my master.

45. Jesus' Lordship over me also means Jesus' Lordship over all evil through me.

46. I become the righteousness of God the moment I am born again and I receive God's nature and eternal life.

47. When I realize my righteousness because of my oneness with God in Christ, demons will fear me as they fear Jesus.

48. Satan trembles and flees when I act fearlessly and confess boldly (Proverbs 28:1; James 4:7; Philippians 1:28)

49. I have become as Jesus was in His earth walk. You reign as a king through Christ. I am master of the kingdom of darkness (1 John 4:17; Romans 5:17)

50. Jesus declared "all power is given to me in heaven and in earth." Jesus said that for my benefit and

empowerment (Matthew 28:18).

51. God's righteousness and justification puts me back in the garden as if sin had never been.

52. Righteousness sets me free from guilt, condemnation, inferiority, inability and insecurity!

53. Righteousness restores my kingdom authority (Hebrews 1:8).

54. Righteousness opens the door for me to have perfect fellowship with God.

55. Righteousness gives me God's divine nature of eternal life.

56. Because of righteousness, I can come confidently into the presence of my holy Father, God Almighty without fear, guilt or insecurity.

57. The fear of the Lord is the key to God's treasures (Isaiah 33:6).

58. I am becoming perfected and established in love.

59. Love perfected in me will cast out all fear and anxiety (1 John 4:18).

60. Perfected love opens my heart and life to the fullness of God (Ephesians 34:19).

61. Love is perfected in me as I practice obeying God's Word (1 John 2:5) and loving people (1 John 4:12).

62. Prayer is my affirmation of dependence on God.

63. Prayer affects the divine, angelic and human realms.

64. Prayer works.

65. Absence of prayer is the forerunner of the absence of power. No prayer; no power!

66. I am true to the real me.

67. I walk in the new man (Ephesians 4:24).

68. I put off the old man (Ephesians 4:22).

69. I put on Christ as my armour (Galatians 3:27).

70. The Bible is not a common book.

71. The Word and God are one.

72. I don't just read about the Word, I feed on the Word! (Jeremiah 5:16).

73. I do more than just reading and listening to the Word. I do the Word and obey the Word. I do what the Word instructs (James 1:22).

Final Word

Jesus said, *"Whosever will save his life shall lose it, but whosoever shall lose his life for my sake and the gospel's shall save it."* (Mark 8:35).

The choice is yours. You can live according to the course of this world's system, do the best you can and have the world's kind of life (Ephesians 2:2). You can live after the flesh and be controlled by its unholy desires and carnal mindedness. You can allow your life to be ruled by your senses and reason without the Holy Spirit. These however all lead to death and problems that arise from sin (Romans 8:5-6).

There is a better way. Choose life! You can have the God kind of life, the abundant life; the life of peace and wholeness. You can be a tree planted by the rivers of water that brings forth its fruit in its season. Your leaf will not wither and whatsoever you do will proper (Psalm 1:3). Storms may come but you can rise above them and they will not blow you down (Matthew 7:25). The Lord will guide you continually and satisfy your soul and make your bones strong. You shall be like a watered garden, and a spring of water whose waters fail not (Isaiah 50:8:11). In days of famine you shall be satisfied (Psalm 37:19).

The Overcomer's Handbook will help establish you in the God kind of life that Jesus wants you to have (John 10:10). Here are 12 principles to help keep you on track and in balance. Use these as a check list to judge yourself from time to time.

1. Matthew 6:33 - Seek first the kingdom of God. Put God first: His will, His purpose, and His ways.

2. Philippians 3:14 - "Press towards the mark for the prize of the high calling of God in Christ Jesus." Pursue intimacy with God as a top priority.

3. I Thessalonians 5:18 - "In every thing give thanks." Maintain an attitude of gratitude.

4. I Thessalonians 5:17 - "Pray without ceasing." Develop and maintain your prayer life.

5. I Thessalonians 5:16 - "Rejoice evermore." Learn to praise and rejoice before God in a manner that pleases Him.

6. Colossians 3:16 - "Let the Word of God dwell in you richly." Spend time in the Word daily.

7. Romans 12:1 - "Present your body a living sacrifice, holy and acceptable unto God."

8. Romans 12:2 - Be transformed by the renewing of your mind. Program your thinking to agree with God's Word.

9. Romans 6:11 - Reckon yourself to be dead to sin. Say no to sin.

10. Matthew 22:37 and 39 - Love the Lord your God with all your heart, and all your soul, and all your mind, and love your neighbour as yourself.

11. Ephesians 4:29 - Let not any corrupt communication proceed our of your mouth. Control your tongue and talk right.

12. Ephesians 5:18 - Be continually filled with the Spirit.

Note: To maximize the effectiveness of this handbook in your life, I ask you to dissect the individual confessions, prayers, and articles. Consider what specific actions you need to take in thought, word, and deed in order to put into practice the truths found in each specific section.

Reminder: Speak the confessions and prayers out loud whenever possible. Faith comes by hearing and hearing the Word of God from your own lips.

Congratulations! You have come to the end of this handbook.

I ask you to take a few additional steps of action:

1. Consider what areas in your life you desire to experience greater development.
2. Consider what areas in your life the Lord is bringing to your attention.
3. Now, re-read this book with these areas in mind, and study the relevant sections. Immerse yourself in the scriptures related until they become real in your heart and your life.

We are in the last days, and the fullness of our salvation is nearer now than ever before. It is my desire to put this handbook into the hands of over a hundred thousand believers.

Psalms 68:11 says, "The Lord gave the Word and great is the company of those who publish it." You can help impact the lives of others by recommending this book to at least two people.

My Prayer for You

I pray that you will be diligent in practicing the things mentioned in this book and that your desire for the Word of God will increase. I pray also that God will perfect everything concerning you and all of His good plan and purpose for your life will be accomplished. I declare in Jesus' name that no weapon formed against you will proper. (2 Peter 1:8-11; Psalm 138:8; Hebrews 13:20 & 21; Isaiah 54:17).

Note: I truly believe that if you invest one hour a day in the pages of this book you will experience more of the victories that belong to you in Christ. Every aspect of your life will be enriched.

Prayer for Salvation

The first step to true success is to become a born again child of God. When you accept Jesus as your Saviour and Lord, you become the righteousness of God in Christ. You will be set free from guilt and condemnation. God will receive you and treat you as if you had never sinned. The kingdom of God will come on the inside of you. God Himself will take up residence in your born again spirit. God becomes your very own Father, and you will take on, His Holy nature. You will have the legal spiritual right to the resources of Heaven and all the promises of God. This will place you in a position where you can be truly successful.

To be born again, you must believe in your heart, that Jesus died for your sins and was raised from the dead, and you must choose Him to be the Saviour and Lord of your life. Say this prayer and mean it with all your heart:

Heavenly Father, I come to you admitting that I am a sinner.

I believe that Jesus died on the cross to take away my sins. I believe that Jesus rose from the dead so that I may be justified and be made righteous. I call upon the name of the Lord Jesus Christ and I ask you Father God to save me and cleanse me from all unrighteousness. I accept Jesus as my Saviour and Lord of my life. I choose to follow you Jesus and live my life for You. I ask you to fill me with the power of the Holy Spirit. I believe I am a born again child of God. I am now the righteousness of God in Christ. Thank You for saving me.

Personal Invitation

● Testimonies

I invite you to share your testimony with me regarding the impact of this book on your life.

Mailing Address: Ian Taylor Ministries Inc.
P.O. Box 69015
Hamilton, Ontario L8K 6R4
E-mail: imtmi@sympatico.ca
Telephone: (905) 549-3884

● Catalogue

Please check out Pastor Ian Taylor's product Catalogue: Tapes, CD's, and DVD's by contacting us at (905)549-3884, or by going to our online store at www.imtmi.com

● Invitation to Partner with us for Come Up Higher in Christ –Television Broadcast

Come Up Higher in Christ is a television program that is broadcasting in parts of Canada, USA, Europe, Africa, India, and Australia through cable, satellite, and the internet. This television program is prophetic, profound, and provocative. It teaches believers how to live out the reality of God dwelling in them. It emphasizes and awakens Christians to the truths of the gift of righteousness, abundance of grace, and the fear of the Lord.

It is my desire to reach this generation on every continent with this message of Come Up Higher in Christ. I invite you to financially partner with me to take this message to every believer everywhere.

You may contact us at:

Mailing address:	Come Up Higher in Christ
	P.O. Box 69015
	Hamilton, Ontario L8K 6R4
	Canada
Telephone:	(905)549-3884
E-mail:	cuhic@sympatico.ca
Website:	www.comeuphigherinchrist.org

Resources

For a complete list of Pastor Ian M. Taylor's product catalogue of: teaching tapes, CD's, TV program DVD's, please call our office, at (905)578-9338, and ask for a copy of the printed catalogue. You may also check our website at www.imtmi.com.

Made in the USA